Landmark
BOOKS

CAPTAIN CORTES CONQUERS MEXICO

By WILLIAM JOHNSON

Illustrated by JOSE CISNEROS

RANDOM HOUSE · NEW YORK

For Jane, Peter and Richard

CONTENTS

APTAIN CORTÉS
ONQUERS MEXICO

y WILLIAM JOHNSON

1519 the remarkable Captain Hernando
ortés led an expedition to Mexico in the
ame of his Spanish king. Mexico at that
me was a vast, unknown country inhab-
ed by fierce, warlike Indians; but there
ere tales of golden treasure and precious
wels to be had for the taking.

The story of the Spanish conquest of
Iexico is as fascinating as any piece of fic-
on, and CAPTAIN CORTÉS CONQUERS
EXICO authentically re-creates this stir-
ng saga of victory and death with all its
rilling swordplay, plunder and violence.
Ve follow the fearless little band of Span-
h adventurers as they make their way
cross jagged mountain ranges, past smok-
g volcanoes, into the dazzling kingdom
f the Aztec Indians. In a gleaming white-
nd-gold city dotted with towering pyra-
ids, blue lakes and floating gardens, the
paniards discover an amazing culture un-
ke anything they have ever known. And
ey meet the powerful ruler of the Aztec
ation, Montezuma, who believes that these
range white men, with their enormous
orses and booming guns, are powerful
ods filled with vengeance.

How a few hundred Spanish warriors,
ith the assistance of a trusted Aztec girl,
cceeded in conquering the stronghold
 an enemy that numbered thousands of
ell-trained fighters is one of history's
ost remarkable episodes. William John-
n's colorful account of this incredible
ue adventure will hold the reader spell-
ound to the very end.

lustrated by JOSE CISNEROS

ANDOM HOUSE, NEW YORK

NEW WORLD WAITING

"CAPTAIN," the young page boy said. "Captain Cortés?"

The thin man with the white face and the black beard turned and looked at the fifteen-year-old boy. Behind him the sea sparkled brightly, and long lines of Indian porters filed past, carrying supplies, manioc bread, live pigs and chickens, bulging sacks, rolls of cloth and casks of wine. They piled them on the deck of a caravel that was tied at the quay.

This was a familiar scene in Cuba in the year 1519. Here were fitted out ships for voyages of discovery to the mysterious lands that lay to the west and north and south of the newly settled West Indies.

One of the porters dropped a box, breaking it, and glass beads—yellow, blue, red and green—scattered on the stone paving of the quay, glistening in the hot sun.

The thin man cursed the porter, speaking in Spanish which the porter did not understand. The porter stooped to pick up the beads. The thin man shrugged his shoulders, twisted the gold loops of his black velvet cloak and finally turned to stare at the page boy.

"I am Captain Hernando Cortés. What do you wish, my son?"

"I am Escobar, a page and your humble servant," said the boy, bowing his head. "I am from the household of his Excellency Don Diego Velásquez, governor of Cuba, and I have a message for you from his Excellency." The boy handed a roll of paper to Cortés. The captain opened the roll, flattened it and frowned as he read it aloud:

> *Esteemed friend and captain:*
>
> Events have made necessary a change in our plans for the expedition to the west. You will, upon receipt of this message, halt all preparations for your voyage, remaining here in Santiago at the orders and command of your governor, VELÁSQUEZ.

"The man is an idiot," said Cortés. "First he orders me to mount an expedition. This I have done, selling my property and borrowing from friends to get funds for ships, soldiers and supplies. Then he changes his mind. He wants an expedition but he wishes me, who has paid for it and organized it, to remain behind. Does he think an expedition will run itself? A great fool . . ."

The page's face was troubled.

"In all respect, sir, I cannot permit you to speak ill of the governor who has been your friend

and my protector and the commander of us both!"

"Ho, listen to the boy! A youth with neither beard nor sword tells me what I shall say."

Escobar stood stiffly straight and said nothing. His eyes did not leave Cortés' face. Finally Cortés smiled.

"You are a good youth. Loyalty is a beautiful thing, no matter where it is placed—or misplaced. Forget what I said, my son. I apologize for speaking ill of Don Diego. We are old friends, and we differ as old friends do. Come along with me. We will sit in the shade and I will compose an answer."

Escobar followed Cortés to a palm-thatched building at the side of the quay. Here, sheltered from the tropical sun, it was cooler; a sea breeze drifted through the reed walls. A barefoot Indian woman placed a glass of wine before Cortés. She also brought a quill pen and a pot of ink.

"Now let us see . . . what shall I tell the governor?" said Cortés, taking a sip of the wine. "I remember you in Don Diego's house. Are you his kinsman?"

"No, sir. I am an orphan. My father came from Spain to Hispaniola with Don Diego, but there my parents died and Don Diego took me into his household."

"I too came here from Hispaniola with Don Diego," said Cortés. "Oh, the gold we thought we would find! Gold we found, but sadly little, and that of poor quality. Now, where we are going— but that does not answer the governor's letter." He started writing with the quill pen, then paused, frowned and brushed his nose with the feather.

"How old are you?" Cortés asked.

"Fifteen, sir."

"A good age," said Cortés. "In Medellín, in the province of Estremadura, when I was a boy I dreamed of wars and conquest and valor at arms. But I was a sickly child, not straight and strong as you are. So I was sent to the great school at Salamanca to learn to be a man of law. But with books I was never content, never. I dreamed always of glory and a soldier's life.

"If I were a fifteen-year-old in Cuba in the year 1519, and if there were a new world waiting in the west, and if some gentlemen and soldiers were mounting an expedition for that new land— I would be with them."

Escobar was silent.

"I know that the governor must have promised you an assignment of land in Cuba when you come of age and an allotment of Indians to work the land."

"Yes, and . . ." said the boy, but Cortés interrupted him.

"And you will scratch these barren hills for gold and, finding little, you will turn to farming. You will live like a peasant. The Indians will steal from you, and they will die, for the devils are unaccustomed to work. You will never have enough Indians to do the work and make you rich. Where we go there will be gold and glory. And having conquered the new land we will, one day, return to Spain to be welcomed as heroes and wealthy men.

"Now your loyalty has struck me. You are the sort of youth I should like to have with me."

"But sir," the boy protested, "the governor has ordered you not to go."

"No matter. He will change his mind. And when we have conquered the new land he will be proud that he allowed us to go. Why, two of his closest friends are going with me, Juan Velásquez de Leon and Diego de Ordaz. The governor will grumble, but he will not stop us. Come with us if you like. Soon you can cease being a page and a future farmer and become a soldier with us." Cortés finished writing his note, waved the paper to dry the ink, and handed it to Escobar.

"My compliments to Don Diego," he said. "And if you decide to join us, we sail tonight, the wind and tide being favorable."

II

A FAREWELL

GOVERNOR DIEGO VELÁSQUEZ was sitting under a flowering tree in his courtyard, playing idly with a small green parrot which was perched on one of his fat fingers. Although he had once been a vigorous soldier, the governor had in recent years become very fat. A thin Cuban Indian stood slightly behind his chair, waving a fan and a fly whisk.

Escobar walked into the courtyard, bowed slightly to the governor and handed him Cortés' message. The governor shook the parrot off his finger and unrolled the paper and squinted at the writing.

"So," he said, sighing heavily, "the man will go whether I will it or not. Had I not all the responsibility of governing this poor, fever-ridden island I would take the expedition myself. But we shall see. When he has found gold in this new land, then will be the time for me to assert my authority. What else did he say?"

"He asked me to come with him," said Escobar.

"And what did you tell him."

"I said nothing."

"But you would like to go?"

"Yes, sir, I would. But I do not wish to offend you."

The parrot fluttered back to the governor's finger, and the fat man stroked its glossy head.

"It is only natural for a youth to want strange lands and adventure," he said, finally. "I did myself at your age. I still do, and I would go on this expedition were it not for my responsibility.

"Go, if you will. You are nearly a man and it is time you learned the profession of arms. In that, Cortés will be a good teacher. But he is not to be trusted in other things. I trust him not; neither should you. Be watchful for ways in which Cortés may try to betray me. My kinsman Juan Velásquez de Leon and my friend Diego de Ordaz will be going too. Them you may trust, and to them you must tell anything you may learn of Cortés' treacherous ways. Tell them whatever Cortés may do against me, in word or deed."

The old governor pulled himself to his feet and told Escobar to follow him. They walked through the big, plain rooms of the governor's residence and into his bedroom. The governor opened a wooden cabinet and after searching for a few minutes he brought out a sword and an old velvet doublet.

"The sword is short and light, but it is of good Toledo steel, a weapon you can carry and use with pride. This doublet was mine in the years before I became so heavy, when I was more nearly your size in the shoulders and chest."

Escobar shrugged his way into the doublet. It was old and worn, and it was far too large for him. He fastened the sword to his belt and practiced drawing it from the scabbard. Then he went to his room and began getting together such possessions as he would need.

At midnight Juan Velázquez de Leon came to tell the governor good-by, and he agreed to take Escobar with him to the quay. He rode a big-boned gray mare. The mare's tail was cut short and she was called Rabona, meaning bobtail. Leon mounted and helped Escobar climb up behind him. They rode off through the dark streets, the sound of the horse's hoofs muffled in the dust.

"A horse," Juan Velásquez was saying, "will be more valuable than a company of infantry. When we came to this island from Hispaniola the Indians were more frightened of our horses than they were of the armed men. They knew naught of horses and thought them some strange gods that were aiding us. I hope that you will help me care for Rabona. I do not mean that you will be a groom; you will be another soldier like the rest of us. I will teach you to use your new sword and I will see to it that you get a soldier's share of whatever treasures we find."

III

THE FLEET SAILS

WHEN CORTES left Santiago, which lies at the eastern end of the island of Cuba, there were only three small ships in his fleet.

The little fleet proceeded slowly along the southern shore of Cuba. At each port it was joined by more ships and more adventurers. Some came with a horse and servant and loads of supplies. Some came only with the clothing they wore and the sword they carried at their side. Some were old and limping, some were little more than children. Many of them had been on earlier voyages to the west.

There had been two earlier expeditions. One, headed by Hernández de Córdova, had gone out in 1517 in search of slaves and had touched at the new land at several points. The second, headed by Juan de Grijalva in 1518, had explored the coast, fought several skirmishes with the Indians, and

managed to send back a supply of golden ornaments and jewels. Some members of the Grijalva
expedition had returned only a few days before
and were ready to go on the new voyage, convinced that much greater riches were to be won
in the new land.

Eight days after sailing from Santiago the fleet
anchored at Cape San Antonio. Here the western
tip of Cuba pointed off toward the west where they
were all bound. There were, by now, eleven ships,
great and small, new and old.

Everyone went ashore. Cortés stretched a can-
opy between two trees and under it he placed a
table. Outside, he set up his standard, a black velvet pennant with a red cross surrounded by blue
and white flames and the motto: "Friends, let us
follow the Cross and under this sign, if we have
faith, we shall conquer."

Seated at his table, Cortés studied the crudely
drawn charts of the new land. Little was known of
it. Men who had been on the earlier voyages came
and spoke with him, and so did the pilots who
would steer the ships. The most experienced of
them was Anton de Alaminos, who came from
Palos in Spain, home of many of the great navi-
gators. Alaminos had been on many voyages and
had served with Columbus on his last voyage, during which they had skirted the coast of Yucatán
where Cortés wished to go now.

Outside in the hot sun, members of the expedition cleaned their armor and swords, rubbing
them with fine sand. Those who owned horses ex-
ercised them in preparation for the inactivity of the
sea voyage.

Finishing his study of the charts, Cortés ordered a review of his forces. There were 553 soldiers. Of these, sixteen were mounted on their own horses. Thirty-two were armed with crossbows. Thirteen carried arquebuses or muskets. There were ten small cannon. This was the total of the fighting force. There were, in addition, 110 sailors and several hundred Cuban Indian servants.

Cortés climbed on a boulder, held out his arms for silence and spoke to his followers.

"Ahead of us lies a land of darkness and of danger. But it is also a land in which we can win glory that will make our names live through the ages. There are grand prizes to be won, but they will not be won with ease. We face hardship and toil, possibly bloodshed and death.

"I have staked all on this venture—my property, my good name and the trust of my friends. And I am willing to spend life itself for the future that awaits us. Follow me, brothers; obey my commands and I will make you masters of a world undreamed of. The Almighty, always with us in our battles against the infidels, will be our shield again. Our cause is just and we will fight under the banner of the cross."

The men shouted approval of their leader's speech and clapped each other on the back. A black-robed priest moved forward and said prayers for the safety of the expedition.

The horses were loaded on the ships again, and soon the whole force was out on the silent sea, moving slowly westward.

Escobar had found two other boys, pages like himself, who had joined the expedition. One was

Orteguilla, from the settlement of Macaca, and the
other was Salazar, who had joined them at Trinidad. The three of them stood together at a ship's
rail, watching the darkening sea and talking of the
review at Cape San Antonio.

"Was it not a fine, brave, beautiful sight?"
asked Escobar. "The soldiers, the flags, the shining

armor, the fine horsemen. Certainly no savages in
the world can stand before an army such as this."

"With such a force as this we will surely conquer and return soon," said Orteguilla. "I should
like to be back in Macaca for my mother's saint's
day and bring her a fine gift of gold."

A big-bodied man with a full brown beard

was standing near them at the rail, staring out at the sea. He turned and spoke to them.

"I should not set my heart upon returning soon, my young friends. We may be gone a long time. We are a fine company of brave men, it is true, and one Spanish fighting man is worth many hundreds of Indians in battle. But remember this. In the land where we are bound the savages are not like the savages you knew in Cuba. In Cuba they were easily conquered—a few shots with cannon and musket, a few charges of the cavalry, and it was all over. Their fighting qualities were no more substantial than the huts in which they lived —huts of thatch and reed that a man could push over with one hand.

"But in New Spain, as we of Grijalva's expedition called it, the savages are different. They build their houses and temples of stone, and some of them are as fine as anything to be seen in Spain or Italy. And their hearts, too, are like stone.

"When we came before to this new land, this New Spain," the man went on, "we made a landing on an island which we called Las Mujeres, the women, because there we found hideous stone figures of women. You have never, my sons, seen such ugliness. But, more important, we could look from the island across a channel toward the mainland. There on the mainland was a city of a magnificence that you cannot imgine—towers and walls of stone, all very grand. Then, when we fought the battle at Cape Catoche, we found that these savages, unlike the Cubans, could fight valiantly and well. They are a fiercer and a nobler race than anything we have found before.

"They wear an armor made of quilted cotton, close-packed, which will stop an arrow or a blow from a pike. It will not stop a dart from a crossbow or a shot from a musket or cannon, nor, for that matter, will it stop a well-muscled blow with good Toledo steel. But the savages have no crossbows, nor muskets, nor cannon, nor Toledo steel. They fight with arrows, darts and spears and strange swords made of wood with edges of polished, sharpened stone. And what a noise the devils make when they attack, blowing whistles and thumping drums and screaming like the foul fiends of hell. Warfare in New Spain is not pleasant, nor is it quick and easy."

The man suddenly stopped talking, but continued to stare out at the sea. Occasionally lights could be seen from the other ships. The wind was picking up; the air was colder and the ship was rolling deeply on the long swells of the open sea. Finally Escobar stretched himself on the deck to sleep. But for a long time be lay awake, shivering, and he did not know whether it was from the freshening wind or the soldier's tales of New Spain.

IV

THE CASTAWAYS

WEST AND SOUTH of Cuba lies the peninsula of Yucatán. Off the east coast of Yucatán lies an island called Cozumel, and this was to be the first landing point for the Spaniards.

Although the ships had tried to stay together in the voyage from Cuba, a gale had separated them. The ship that Cortés himself commanded had to go back and take in tow another ship that had been disabled.

The first ship to drop anchor in the harbor at Cozumel was one commanded by Pedro de Alvarado. Alvarado was one of four brothers who had joined the expedition at Trinidad. All were veterans of the Grijalva expedition.

Pedro de Alvarado was a tall, broad-shouldered man with hair and beard the color of a shiny copper coin. His voice was loud and his manner bold. Landing at Cozumel he immediately led a

small group of his men into a nearby village, seiz-
ing what food supplies he could find and driving
the Indians away. He ransacked the local temple
for the few gold ornaments it contained and returned to the shore.

Cortés' ship was the last to arrive. When Cortés came ashore he went to inspect the village.

"But where are the people who live in this
village?" he asked.

When he heard what Alvarado had done,
Cortés frowned and summoned the big red-headed
man. He asked him if it were true that he had
stolen from the natives and driven them from their
homes.

"Steal from them, my captain?" asked Alvarado. "One does not steal from natives. A Spanish
gentleman takes from the heathen whatever he
needs. That is not stealing. That is the right and
privilege of a conqueror."

"Alvarado, I know you are a brave man,"
said Cortés. "Otherwise I would not have allowed
you to join us. But bravery is of little account un-
less it is tempered by judgment. Of that you have
shown little. By all accounts the natives of this
place are friendly. Yet you seize their property and
frighten them away.

"Look, friend Alvarado. There will be times for
bravery and times for judgment. This was a time
for judgment. If we can make our way in this land
with friendship, that is the way we will do it."

Cortés then ordered that the stores of food and
the temple ornaments taken by Alvarado be spread
out on the ground before the village. When the
natives stared at them through the trees, the Span-

iards gestured to them to approach and take back their belongings. The Indians finally came near and, finding that the Spaniards would not harm them, brought gifts of meat, fruit and earthen jars of corn.

Cortés had heard that some white men, survivors of an earlier shipwreck, were held captive by the Indians on the peninsula of Yucatán. He sent search parties across the channel to Yucatán to look for the castaways, but they found nothing.

Finally, after resting and replenishing their supplies of food and water, the Spaniards prepared to leave Cozumel. As they were embarking they saw a large canoe being paddled furiously toward them from the mainland. When it reached the shore a

man who appeared to be an Indian jumped from
the canoe, approached Cortés and threw himself on
the ground.

"Am I among Christians?" he asked, speaking

Spanish. The Spaniards stared at him in amazement. He was nearly naked. His skin was as
brown as an Indian's, and his long black hair was
tied back with a piece of animal skin.

Cortés ssured him that he was and threw his
own cloak around the man's shoulders.

"Who are you and how do you come to be
here?" he asked.

The man said his name was Jerónimo de
Aguilar. He was a Spanish priest who had settled
at Darien in Panama. Eight years before, he had
been in a shipwreck and he and a companion, another Spaniard, had been taken prisoner by the
Indians of Yucatán. Since then they had lived
among the Indians. Aguilar had become the slave
of an Indian chief who treated him kindly and
finally granted him his freedom. His companion,
although he knew of the arrival of the Spaniards,
had chosen to remain among the Indians.

Aguilar was given clothing and made welcome.
He told Cortés he knew the Indian dialects and
customs of the region and that he would be glad
to help the expedition.

The fleet sailed around the tip of the Yucatán
peninsula. The ships did not stop until they came
to an island which sheltered a large bay. Here the
Spaniards anchored and went ashore, looking for
fresh water and game.

Escobar, the page, went with one of the hunting parties. They found a spring of fresh, sweet
water, but there was little game to be seen. Suddenly they heard a sound from far up the beach
ahead of them. Straining their eyes in the brilliant
sunlight, they could see an animal running toward

them at great speed. Then they heard the noise
again; it sounded like a dog's bark. The animal
came closer—it was a dog. It ran to them, jumped
on them, rolled at their feet, crying with pleasure.
It was a greyhound such as many of the men had
known in Spain and Cuba as hunting dogs. But
how did it get to this lonely tropical island?

While the men were wondering about it, the
dog jumped to its feet and ran into the jungle.
The Spaniards called to it, but it did not return.
Still wondering they continued their search for
game.

Then the dog reappeared, carrying a fresh-
killed rabbit. It brought the rabbit to the Spaniards, dropped it at their feet and ran off into the
jungle again. Soon it returned, carrying another
rabbit. This continued until the greyhound had
brought a dozen large rabbits. Then it seemed
content to lie on the sand, staring at the men.
When they returned to the ship it gladly went
along.

At first the dog was a mystery. Then one of
the men recalled that during the Grijalva expedition some of the men had gone ashore on the same
island to hunt for deer. They had taken a greyhound with them, but while the greyhound was
running a deer some Indian warriors had approached. The Spaniards had hastily returned to
their ship, leaving the dog behind.

Escobar took charge of the dog and named
it Cazadora, or huntress.

V

GOLD FROM THE WEST

THE FLEET sailed on around the coast until it came to the mouth of a large river. Near here, Cortés was told, was a town called Tabasco, where the natives had been friendly with the men from the Grijalva expedition.

"May they still be friendly," said Cortés, giving orders to anchor and disembark. Anchor chains rattled, sails were lowered, and the Spaniards prepared to go ashore in small boats.

They soon became aware of Indians watching them from the dense growth along the river banks, and when the small boats approached shore the Indians swarmed out toward them in canoes. But they were not friendly. They brandished spears and tried to upset the Spaniards' boats. Failing this they hurled blazing pieces of wood into the boats, trying to set them afire.

The Spaniards fought back. Their armor protected them from the shower of spears and arrows, and with their pikes they managed to overturn many of the Indian canoes. Finally they reached the shore and struggled up the muddy bank. The Indians slowly retreated and the Spaniards followed them until they came to a town which had been abandoned by the natives. Here Cortés called a halt and ordered a camp to be set up in the courtyard of the principal Indian temple.

In the courtyard stood a big, thick-trunked silk-cotton tree. Calling his men to attention, Cortés took his sword and cut three deep gashes in the trunk.

"Thus I declare," he said, "that this land is now the possession of his majesty Don Carlos, king of Spain. My sword and my shield are ready to defend this title."

His followers cheered and then went back to work, cleaning swords and muskets, checking crossbow cords, sharpening the tips of their pikes.

No one rested. Cortés himself kept on the move, talking with his men, checking sentry posts, sending out scouts. The scouts, returning, reported there was a great army of Indians gathered on a plain a few miles away, apparently prepared for battle. Finally deciding that there could be no peaceful settlement, Cortés ordered horses and cannon unloaded from the ships.

Cortés himself took charge of the cavalry, which was to swing around the Indians massed on the plain, while the foot soldiers were to march directly toward them under the command of Diego de Ordaz.

The morning was hot and quiet. The leaves

on the tropical trees hung limp and the Spaniards
sweated uncomfortably under their armor. The foot
soldiers marching toward the plain could not keep
ranks, try as they would. The flat land around the
town was crisscrossed with irrigation ditches, and
the land itself was thick with growing corn and
strange vegetables.

They came to the end of the fields and floun-
dered through one last ditch. Beyond them was the

plain, and massed on it, as far as eye could see, were Indians.

Before the last Spanish foot soldier had climbed out of the ditch, there was a single, piercing scream from the Indians, then the roar of thousands of voices. As the screaming died away, the Spaniards heard a sharp hissing in the air.

"Arrows," they shouted, and at the same time some of them groaned.

Ordaz roared commands at his men. Artillerymen worked furiously to set up their mud-caked cannon, and musketeers checked carefully to see if their powder charges were still dry. The Indians were advancing at a dead run. Arrows and spears continued to fall among the Spaniards, and now the Indians threw rocks as well.

Finally the cannon were ready, and Ordaz gave the order to fire. The little guns roared, and the cannon balls left bloody tracks in the midst of the massed Indians. Musket fire, too, was deadly, but the Indians came rushing on in screaming thousands. Some were nearly naked; some wore white cotton gowns, and others had brilliantly dyed cloaks.

"St. James and St. Peter!" the Spaniards shouted, and plunged into hand-to-hand fighting. The gunfire, the murderous darts of the crossbows and the sharp-edged steel swords gave them an advantage over the primitive weapons of the Indians. But for every Indian the Spaniards struck to the ground, a hundred more seemed to come on. They screamed and shouted, and threw handfuls of dust and dried grass in the air to add to the confusion.

Escobar, the page, had not been in the first ranks of the advancing Spaniards, and at first he was not involved in the fighting. Grasping the sword that the governor had given him, he stared in amazement at his first battle. Suddenly the line ahead of him gave way and a flood of Indians seemed to engulf him. He took a few steps backward and found himself with his back to a tree.

He chopped and thrust with his sword, swinging blindly. One Indian went down in front of him, but there were many more.

Just when it seemed hopeless, there was a change in the Indians' cries. Many of them turned and looked toward the rear. There, at a dead run, came the Spanish horsemen, their armor reflecting the hot sun, their lances leveled. The Indians screamed with fright, dropped their weapons and ran.

"See," shouted Ordaz, "the infidels think horse and rider are one great animal, the like of which they have never seen. Thanks be to St. James and St. Peter! Forward!"

The foot soldiers sprang into the mass of Indians, thrusting and hacking with their swords, and the Indians climbed over one another in their desperate flight.

Soon the battle was over and the battlefield strangely silent. The Spanish horsemen pursued the fleeing Indians for a short distance but then returned to where the foot soldiers were waiting, still breathing heavily and looking at the body-strewn field. Slowly they returned to their camp. Some of the Spaniards were wounded. They sat on the ground and treated their wounds as best they could.

The next morning a delegation of the Tabascan chieftains came to the Spaniards' camp. Following them was a long line of porters who carried jars and baskets of food as gifts.

Using Aguilar as an interpreter, Cortés welcomed them gravely.

The spokesman for the Tabascans said he wished to apologize for the attack on the Spaniards.

"But why," asked Cortés, "did you attack us when you were friendly with the other white men who came here?"

Because, said the Tabascans, a great ruler who lived in the west had criticized them for being friendly with strangers.

"And where does this great ruler live?" asked Cortés.

In Mexico, the Tabascans said, in his capital, called Tenochtitlán.

The Tabascans then brought forward more gifts, some female slaves and a box of gold trinkets.

Cortés examined the gold. It was not of good quality, but it was gold, and gold was what they were seeking.

He asked the Tabascans if they had gold mines. They said that they did not.

Where, then, Cortés asked, did the gold come from?

"From Mexico," they said. "From Tenochtitlán." And again they pointed toward the west.

VI

THE SPIES

UNKNOWN TO the Spaniards, two observers had watched their battle and the victory over the Tabascans.

The two were Aztecs, taller and stronger and thinner of face than the Tabascans. They were spies for the great Aztec ruler, Montezuma. The kingdom of the Aztecs, called Mexico, was far away to the west and north, in a high mountain valley.

One of the spies rapidly drew pictures of the battle on a long roll of rough paper. He faithfully sketched the armored Spaniards, their ships, their horses, cannon, guns and crossbows, adding symbols for numbers. He showed in detail how the Spanish cavalry had routed the Tabascans.

The other Aztec spy took the roll of paper, placed it carefully in a deerskin pouch and tied the pouch to his back. He then started running, following faint paths in the jungle, racing along

beaches, fording or swimming the rivers and
streams that emptied into the ocean. By sundown
he had left the coast and had begun to climb toward the plateaus, beyond which lay ranges of
mountains. Finally he came to a clearing where
two other Aztecs sat on the ground by a small fire.
One of the two jumped to his feet, took the deerskin pouch from the weary runner and sped off
into the dark, running toward the west.

Two days later a fleet-footed man raced down
into the valley of Mexico. Behind him was a tremendous range of mountains. Two of the mountain
peaks were covered with snow, and from one of
them arose a plume of smoke, pink-tinted in the
morning light.

Ahead and below him lay the great valley. In
the center of the valley was a lake, really a group
of five smaller lakes which joined one another. The

water reflected the blue of the sky. And in the center of the lake there was a great city, criss-crossed with canals and connected with the mainland by three long causeways.

This was Tenochtitlán, capital of the Aztecs and the most powerful city in all of the land. It was to remain the capital, now known as Mexico City.

The runner raced down from the highlands and along the causeway leading to the city from the southeast. Anchored in the water on either side of the causeway were floating gardens or small man-made islands that looked like huge rafts covered with earth on which grew vegetables and flowers. Canoes glided between the islands, gathering produce, and then skimmed lightly over the surface of the lake toward the city, a great cluster of buildings, some of them pure white, some a dull red. Reaching into the sky above the other buildings were pyramids, many of them; and from the summits of the pyramids rose pillars of smoke.

The runner reached the city, crossed the central plaza and halted at the entrance to a long, low building of red stone. He spoke breathlessly with a guard who wore a cloak of red and green feathers and a helmet fashioned of copper and green stone. He handed the guard the deerskin pouch and collapsed on the stone pavement, his head in his arms.

The guard removed the roll from the pouch and walked hurriedly through a series of rooms, each more splendidly decorated than the last. He stopped before a cluster of men who sat cross-legged on the floor before a screen of gold and silver. Their feathered cloaks were more finely made than that of the guard, and their elaborate helmets resembled the heads of wild animals. One of the men took the roll from the guard. Removing his feathered cloak, his headdress and his sandals, he drew around himself a plain, coarse cloak of cotton and, with his head bowed, went behind the screen and through a portal.

The room was long and high-ceilinged. The stone floors were covered with finely embroidered cloths. Thick draperies were drawn back and embrasures in the thick walls were open to the morning sunlight, looking out on a garden of brilliant flowers.

Two men were seated at a low table. One wore severe black robes. The other wore a cloak of white cotton trimmed with blue; on his head was a golden crown and on his feet were golden sandals.

Servants passed before them with pottery trays of food, whole roasted birds and pigs, baskets of thin corn cakes, bowls heaped high with fruits. The two men paid little attention to the food but talked together in low tones.

The courtier approached, walking slowly with his head bowed. He stopped before the man in the white robe.

"My lord," he said, and bowed low.

"My great lord," he said, and bowed again.

"My great lord Montezuma," he said, and bowed even lower, remaining in a bowed position.

"Rise and speak," said the man in the white robe.

"A message has come from the hot country of

the rising sun, the land of the Tabascans," said the courtier, and handed Montezuma the scroll.

Montezuma took the paper and carefully unrolled it. As his eyes followed the drawings telling of the battle and the Spaniards' victory, he frowned He looked through the scroll again, handed it to his companion, and stared into the garden.

The man in the black robe studied the scroll in silence. Finally Montezuma spoke:

"In the age of the wind-sun the Feathered Serpent god came among us bringing learning and culture. But when our people showed that they were not ready for his teachings he went away to the place where the sun rises beyond the ocean, saying that he would some day return.

"Three times these fair-skinned strangers have landed on our shores, two summers ago, one summer ago, and now. Their skins are white, as was that of the Feathered Serpent god. They have come from the direction of the sun's rising. They come in houses that have wings and fly upon the water. They carry with them great animals like deer, but very much larger with no antlers, and the deer carry the men into battle. They have weapons that kill with fire and smoke.

"Tell me, brother priest, could this be what the Feathered Serpent god prophesied for us. Is he angry because we neglect him in worship, since we make our sacrifies to the Smoking Mirror god and the Hummingbird Wizard god instead?"

The priest thought for a moment, ran a long thin hand through his dark hair, and replied:

"Lord Montezuma, our gods are difficult to understand. But I doubt that these white-faced

strangers come from the Feathered Serpent god.
The Tabascans are not great warriors as we Aztecs
are great. Yet the arrows and knives of the Tabascans drew blood from these strangers. If they were
gods or the children of a god this could not happen."

Montezuma frowned. "Perhaps we do not clearly
see that which the gods intend for us to see. But
there have been many omens. We Aztecs have
ruled with strength and zeal. We have made vassal states of the kingdoms around us; we rule the
country from the ocean of the morning sun to the
ocean of the evening sun. We sacrifice our prisoners
to the Hummingbird Wizard and the Smoking
Mirror. But we have not done this without making
enemies. There are jealous men and jealous gods.

"I am troubled by the omens. The high waves
in the lake that surrounds us. The smoke and
flame that we see by night in the eastern sky. Our
temples destroyed by strange fires. At night I hear
a woman's voice calling, 'My children, my children,
we are lost.' And only yesterday my hunters
brought me a strange fowl they had captured.
Mounted on its head, instead of plumage, there
was a mirror. And looking in this mirror I saw, not
my face, but the stars in the sky. And then these
stars changed to strange, warlike men."

When Montezuma had finished speaking, the
priest looked at the floor in silence, then reached
for a small gold pipe filled with tobacco and incense, lighted it with a blazing pine splinter and
smoked in silence. Montezuma, frowning slightly,
continued to stare into the garden. Finally Montezuma turned to the priest again.

"Since we cannot know whether they are god-like creatures or mortal men and enemies, we will treat them as both. We will send them rich gifts, rich enough for gods, so that they will know me for the religious and wealthy king that I am. But we will also send them away. With the gifts which I will send to them they should leave gladly."

VII

MALINCHE

THE SPANISH fleet left Tabasco and, in fair spring weather, glided along the coast of the new land, moving toward the west. They passed the mouths of great rivers and could see high mountain ranges far inland. One of the peaks was covered with snow, and in the early morning hours, while the rest of the land was dark, it was the first to catch the rays of the rising sun, glistening like a ruby.

Finally they anchored off an island which earlier voyagers had named San Juan de Ulua, near the present-day port of Vera Cruz. They were no sooner anchored than large canoes loaded with Indians swept out toward them from the sandy mainland. The Spaniards, remembering Tabasco, readied their weapons. Then, as the Indians drew nearer, the explorers could see that they were unarmed.

The largest of the canoes contained two Indians more elaborately costumed than the rest. They carried staves decorated with red and green feathers. This canoe made for Cortés' ship, and the paddlers helped the two chieftains to climb the railing.

Cortés was waiting for them, standing stiff and straight and wrapped in his black velvet cloak, although the day was hot. The chieftains approached him and bowed low. Servants following them swung silver pots from which incensed smoke billowed.

Cortés returned their bow, and one of the Indians began speaking.

"Come, Aguilar, and tell me what he is saying," Cortés ordered.

Aguilar listened to the chieftain, shrugged his shoulders and said: "I do not understand, my captain. It is a strange tongue. I know only the Mayan language of Tabasco and Yucatán."

On the forward deck of the ship stood the Indian women slaves whom the Tabascans had given to Cortés. One, the handsomest of the lot, walked back to where Cortés and the Indian chieftains stood. She spoke with one of the chieftains. He nodded and began speaking rapidly with many gestures, pointing frequently toward the west.

The Indian woman turned and spoke to Aguilar in the Mayan language, and Aguilar repeated it to Cortés in Spanish.

"They are emissaries," said Aguilar, "sent by the ruler of this region, who is an ally of Montezuma, Aztec king of Mexico. On behalf of their lord and of Montezuma they bid us welcome and ask what we may need in the way of provisions, which they hope they can supply."

Cortés smiled and told Aguilar to express his thanks. He ordered food and drink brought for the emissaries. When they had eaten he reached in a leather pouch and brought out a handful of blue glass beads which he gave to the Indians. The Indians examined them closely, thanked him and left, promising to return.

The Spaniards disembarked and went to the mainland to set up a camp in the sand dunes. Almost immediately Indians came to the camp, bringing carcasses of deer, wild pigs, fowl, strange fruits and vegetables and corn. Others brought gifts for Cortés, trinkets of gold, precious stones, cloaks made of feathers and bolts of finely woven white cloth.

After discovering that she knew the language of this land, Cortés kept the Indian woman near him for all conversations with the natives. He gave her the name of Marina, a name which sounded something like her Indian name, Malinche. Because she was always at his side the Indians came to address Cortés as Malinche, too.

Cortés asked Aguilar to learn her history and how she happened to speak this language as well as that of the Tabascans.

"It is a strange story, my captain," Aguilar reported. "As a child she lived in a place not far from here. That country and this are subject to the rule of the Aztecs, and as a child she spoke in the Aztec tongue. Her father was a chieftain, a wealthy one. But her father died and her mother remarried. The stepfather wanted the dead prince's wealth for himself, but Marina was entitled to a share of it. Then the daughter of one of his slaves died, a child about Marina's age. The stepfather sold Ma-

rina to some traveling traders and buried the slave's daughter, telling his friends and neighbors that it was Marina. The traders sold the child to the Tabascans, and she grew to womanhood among them. Thus she knows this strange Aztec language and also the Mayan language which I know.

"Mark my words, my captain, she will be of great importance to your venture. She is a woman of intelligence and delicacy, and she knows not only the Aztec tongue but the Aztec heart and mind as well."

When the Spaniards had been ashore a week they were visited by the ruler of the region. His name was Teuhtile and he came to the Spaniards' camp carried in a litter borne by warriors.

"I bring the greetings of my lord Montezuma," said Teuhtile. "It has been his pleasure to welcome you to this land and to order that you be supplied with food and other necessities. I go now to visit my lord Montezuma. If you have any message for him, I shall take pleasure in being your messenger."

"Tell him," said Cortés, "that we have come from a great king across the sea who wishes to be his friend. And that we, as ambassadors of our great king, wish to come and see him and pay our respects in person."

Teuhtile shook his head doubtfully. Montezuma, he said, would not consent to an interview.

Cortés then brought out gifts for Teuhtile to deliver to Montezuma; a cape of red cloth, some European shirts and an intricately carved wooden chair.

"May he wear these and sit in this chair when we come to see him."

Teuhtile again shook his head, but promised to deliver both the gifts and the message.

Several times during the conversation Teuhtile had glanced at a soldier who stood near by.

"May I see that man's helmet?" he asked finally. The helmet was handed to him. It was a steel helmet of curious shape, and it had been gilded.

"It is very much like the helmet worn by our Feathered Serpent god when he went across the eastern sea, leaving us. May I take it to show to my lord Montezuma?"

"Yes," said Cortés, "on one condition."

"And what is that?"

"That when you return, you bring it filled with the gold dust of your country; I should like to compare it with the gold of our own country."

Teuhtile left. And as he left, the Spanish soldiers who had listened to the interview nudged one another and winked slyly.

Within a fortnight Teuhtile returned. Behind him came a procession of one hundred heavily laden porters. The Indian chieftain entered Cortés' tent. Attendants waved their incense pots in the air, perfuming it, while others unrolled reed mats on the ground. The porters then paraded through, each placing his load on the mats.

The Spaniards could hardly believe their eyes. There were two huge plates, as large as cart wheels, one of gold, one of silver. There was the old Spanish helmet that Teuhtile had borrowed, brimming over with grains of gold. There were gold figures of animals, birds and fish, gold ornaments, piles of shining green stones, carefully wrought golden figures of men and gods, and quantities of finely made cloth.

Cortés exclaimed over the magnificence of the gifts and thanked Teuhtile.

"And what," he asked, "about the interview with Lord Montezuma?"

Teuhtile drew himself up stiffly and replied: "There will be no interview. My lord Montezuma says that if your king should come to these shores he would be glad to receive him in person. But he thinks that you, having visited this country, should

now return to your own and take these gifts to your king."

Saying this, Teuhtile left, somewhat haughtily.

One of the soldiers who had watched the meeting asked, half to himself, if this meant that the Spaniards would go home now.

Pedro de Alvarado grinned broadly through his red beard.

"Ha!" he exclaimed. "Go back now when we've just found where the gold comes from? Do you get up from the table after a single bite of food? Look at our captain. Does he look like a man about to leave?"

Cortés, with Marina close behind him, was kneeling before the helmet, letting the grains of gold trickle through his fingers.

VIII

ALL TIES CUT

AFTER THE SECOND visit of Teuhtile the Indians, who had generously supplied the Spaniards with food, suddenly stopped coming to the camp.

Within a few days the Spaniards were critically short of food. The sailors went out in their boats to fish, but they could not bring in enough to feed the camp. Other Spaniards ranged through the sand dunes looking for game, but there was little of it.

Many of them, too, had begun to suffer from fever. Wounds received in the battle of Tabasco were slow in healing, and a number of the men died.

Some of the close friends of Diego Velásquez thought that the expedition should return to Cuba with the treasures they had won, so that the governor might have his share. Cortés, on the other hand, insisted that they remain in New Spain,

found a colony and eventually march to Tenochtitlán, the Aztec capital.

Leaders of the opposition were Juan Velásquez
de Leon and Diego de Ordaz. Late one night they
awakened Escobar, the page.

"Come, boy," said Leon. "We are going before Cortés to demand that we return to Cuba.
There will be a count of hands for those who wish
to return. We need you."

Escobar followed them obediently to a blazing
fire around which all members of the expedition
had gathered. Cortés stood within the circle.

Pedro de Alvarado was on his feet, speaking.

"I remind you, my brothers, of what happened to us of the Grijalva expedition. I remember
it well for it was I who was chosen to take back
to Cuba the shipload of treasure from these shores.
The treasure was seized by our fat governor, Diego
Velásquez. He did, it is true, send one fifth of it
on to Spain as the king's share. But what did he
do with the rest of it? Did any of it go to Juan
de Grijalva who led our expedition? Was any of it
divided among those of us who made up the expedition? You know the answer. Not one peso!"

Leon leaped to his feet.

"This is treason," he shouted. "We are here
only on the authority of Diego Velásquez who is
the king's agent. Disloyalty to the governor is disloyalty to his majesty the king!"

"Let me finish," said Alvarado. "Then we shall
speak of disloyalty. I say that our work here is un-
finished. We have had a sample of the wealth of
Tenochtitlán, the riches of this heathen emperor,
Montezuma. Now that we know who has the

treasure, we should go and sit by his side and pull his beard and forget this childish wish to return to Cuba. The adventure is only well started.

"This afternoon I have surveyed the site where we are camped. Upon it we could build a little town, a fortress, a retreat in case of adversity. I propose that we do this, and that we establish a government for our colony. And this government would be dedicated to serving his majesty Don Carlos. And hereafter we would deal directly with Spain instead of Cuba and that thieving governor, Diego Velásquez!"

There was a great shout from the circle of men, some applauding Alvarado, others protesting.

"Outrage!" shouted Leon.

"One little moment more," said Alvarado, his hands raised. "For this settlement, we must elect a captain general to be the supreme authority in New Spain, his majesty's representative, leader in battles, dispenser of justice, defender of our holy religion. There is only one choice for such a post— the man who has thus far led us ably and well and has pointed the way to greater success, our captain, Don Hernando Cortés!"

Again there were shouts from the circle of men. Under Alvarado's direction those who supported his plan filed to one side of the fire; those who favored a return to Cuba and Diego Velásquez went to the other. Some of the men stood midway, trying to make up their minds. But finally all went over to Alvarado's side except three: Juan Velásquez de Leon, Diego de Ordaz and Escobar the page.

Cortés was being congratulated by his men,

but then he separated himself from them and approached the three who were opposed to him.

"Will you not change your minds?" he asked.

Leon and Ordaz said nothing and slowly walked away.

Puzzled, Escobar returned to the tree under which he had made himself a bed. Cazadora, the greyhound, nuzzled his hand. When the boy finally went to sleep, his arm was around the dog's neck.

In the morning he walked out into the dunes with the dog. She scented a rabbit, dashed away through the scrubby brush and presently brought the animal and dropped it at Escobar's feet. He returned to the camp, built himself a fire, cut up the rabbit and roasted it over the coals.

While he was gnawing on the bones, a shadow fell across him. He looked up. It was Cortés. Escobar jumped to his feet.

"Remain seated, my son," said Cortés. "I am sure you are troubled by what happened last night. As I told you before, your loyalty to Don Diego Velásquez was the thing that attracted me to you in the first place.

"I wanted to tell you that I have spoken with Leon and Ordaz, both of whom are fine, brave soldiers. And they have changed their minds. I have shown them how we can better serve our king by continuing our present course. And naturally," and he smiled, "we can at the same time better serve ourselves.

"I hope that you, too, will see this. And I should like to propose another thing. As captain general of New Spain, I have need of personal attendants. I have already asked your friends, Orteguilla and Salazar, to serve as my pages. Pages are necessary, but I have a more important post for you if you will accept it.

"I need a chamberlain, one who will see to it that my headquarters, wherever it may be, runs smoothly; who will supervise Indian servants and give instructions to the pages."

He paused and looked at Escobar closely. Escobar stared at the ground.

"And as our treasures accumulate," Cortés continued, "you will see that they are secure and accounted for. But, above all, you will continue to be a soldier for Spain."

IX

THE FAT CHIEF

HAVING SETTLED the unrest among his followers, Cortés next moved to get them out of the un-
healthy, barren coastal region. Plans for building a
town on the campsite were dropped.

Scouts had reported that there was a safer anchorage for the ships a short distance to the north.
Cortés ordered the fleet to move to the new loca-
tion while he and his men marched overland. He
wanted to visit a town called Cempoala. Strange
Indians had come into the camp, different in ap-
pearance from the Aztecs of the region. Questioned,
they said they were Totonacs. Their capital was
Cempoala, a few days' march to the northwest.
They had been conquered by the Aztecs in years
past and had been forced to pay tribute to Montezuma. But they liked neither Montezuma nor the
tax collectors he sent among them to exact tribute.

Cortés and his men marched off, struggling

through the deep sand of the dunes and the dense brush that grew farther inland. Trees became larger and, away from the salt breeze of the ocean, the air became sweet with the fragrance of strange flowers and ferns. In valleys they saw deer grazing, and here and there were cultivated fields of corn.

On the third day of marching they were met by a group of twelve Indians who offered to lead them to Cempoala. Cautious lest they be led into a trap, Cortés ordered his men to march with arms ready, and scouts were sent ahead.

One of the scouts came running back breathlessly and reported to Cortés: "I have seen it, I have seen it! It is a city built all of silver, shining in the sun!"

The Spaniards nudged one another and resumed their march at a faster pace. Finally, from the crest of a hill, they looked down upon the town. It seemed large and well-built, with many great buildings, broad streets and gardens of flowers. The buildings did shine in the sun, but they were not silver. They were painted with white lime.

A large group of Indians approached, holding garlands of flowers. As the Spaniards drew near, the Indians draped the flowers around the soldiers' necks and led the way into the city. The Indians were splendidly dressed in white robes. Many wore ornaments of gold in their noses and ears.

The white men were led through the streets and into a large courtyard which, they were told, was to be their home for as long as they liked. Indian women came with baskets of corn cakes and fresh plums. The Spaniards, weary from the long march and hungry for days, devoured the food.

"Why do they treat us so well, my captain?" asked Escobar.

"I think we shall learn that presently," replied Cortés. "See who comes."

Into the courtyard came a group of Indians, apparently chieftains. In their midst was a huge fat man. His embroidered cloak was much richer than the rest. Buttons of gold were fastened in his lower lip and in his ears. Around his thick neck was a string of small plates of gold. His legs were the size of wine casks. He moved slowly and as he did so his huge stomach shifted from side to side. Attendants held each arm to help him walk.

The fat chief greeted Cortés and asked his mission.

"We have come from across the sea," said Cortés, "as emissaries of a great king who wishes you well. Our king loves justice and hates cruelty. Is there anything that we can do to serve you?"

The fat man sighed, wheezing heavily.

"We Totonacs are no longer our own masters," he said. "We, and there are thirty towns in my kingdom, have been made a subject people, vassals of the Aztecs. They come among us and take away our gold and jewels, and they carry off the fairest of our children to be sacrificed in the great temples of Tenochtitlán." As he spoke the fat man's eyes filled with tears.

"And what can we do to help you?" asked Cortés.

"The Aztecs are great warriors," said the fat chief. "But you have weapons of magic. You have great canoes that fly on the water with white wings. You have iron dogs that send lightning and

thunder out of their mouths. You have great deer
that carry men into battle on their backs, trampling your enemies under their feet. Even the
heartless Aztecs cannot fight these magic things.
You can protect us from them and we will be
your loyal friends and allies, your servants."

"Perhaps we can help you," said Cortés. He
then told the fat chief that his ships, the great
winged canoes, had sailed up the coast to an anchorage, and that he wished to go there.

"Yes," said the chief, "they have gone to
Chiahuitzla, which is another town in my kingdom. I shall place servants and porters at your
disposal. The town shall be yours, and I myself
will go there with you to make certain that everything pleases you."

The next morning the Spaniards resumed their
march.

As they marched, Cortés spoke with some of
his companions.

"I think," he said, "that with the fortune of
fools and the help of the Almighty we may have
stumbled upon a valuable secret, a key that will
unlock this strange, cruel land and let us bring in
the light of truth and justice.

"The Aztecs are everywhere feared and no-
where loved. Through their cruelty they have conquered. But conquest is followed by hatred, and
where hatred exists, nothing is permanent.

"Some of you must have wondered how we,
barely four hundred men, can hope to conquer this
strange land. It is really quite simple. We shall set
Indian against Indian. There must be many other
chiefs with large kingdoms who hate the Aztecs.

We shall bring the light of God to these savages and we shall bring greater glory to our king. And we shall, if it interest you gentlemen, each of us become as rich as lords."

X

DIPLOMACY

IN CHIAHUITZLA the Spaniards unloaded their ships. With the help of native workmen supplied by the fat chief, they set about building a permanent settlement of their own near by.

In the midst of this work the Spaniards were to see how Cortés intended to set Indian against Indian.

Into Chiahuitzla one day came a group of Aztecs. They walked solemnly through the plaza of the town, their embroidered robes floating into the breeze behind them, their ribboned topknots bobbing. In their hands they carried flowers. As they walked they sniffed at the flowers and looked neither to right nor left, ignoring the Spaniards as well as the Totonacs.

A group of Totonac nobles, the fat chief among them, had been clustered around Cortés. They abruptly left, following the Aztecs across the plaza and into a building.

"What is happening?" Cortés asked Marina. "Who are these men?"

Marina spoke rapidly with a Totonac warrior and then explained to Cortés:

"They are, my lord, tax gatherers of the Aztec ruler, Montezuma. They have brought word that Montezuma is displeased with the Totonacs for entertaining and aiding the white men. And as punishment the Totonacs must provide ten young men and ten young women to be sacrificed on the pyramids of Tenochtitlán."

Cortés gave orders for the fat chief to be brought before him. The chief came, quivering with fear of both the Aztecs and the Spaniards.

"You will seize these tax collectors," said Cortés, "and make them prisoners."

When Marina had finished translating what Cortés said, the fat chief's body shook with sobs and tears glided down his cheeks.

"Oh no, Lord Malinche, they would come and kill us all and destroy our cities."

"Are you not our allies?" Cortés asked, sternly. "Do you not want our aid in throwing off the Aztec yoke? You must do as I say."

The fat chief groaned and objected, but he finally called some of his warriors to him and gave them orders in a choking voice.

The surprised Aztecs were thrown into a stone building, protesting loudly and promising disaster for the Totonac kingdom.

"Shall we kill them now?" asked Pedro de Alvarado.

"Friend Alvarado, your disposition is as fiery as your beard. If you will watch closely you will see an exercise in diplomacy. Diplomacy is a greater art than war, and a very necessary art when you are outnumbered as we are."

"Sir, I do not understand," said Escobar, who was standing nearby. "What is diplomacy?"

"It is a type of magic that is better demonstrated than explained," said Cortés. "I will show you."

That night Escobar was awakened. Cortés stood over him.

"Come, boy, and have your lesson in diplomacy."

Escobar arose, rubbed the sleep from his eyes and followed the captain into the room he used as headquarters. Cortés seated himself at a rough table, lighted by a single candle.

There was a noise outside, feet shuffling and armor clinking. The Aztec tax collectors, their arms tied behind their backs, were led into the room by Spanish soldiers. The Aztecs were still haughty, but there was a look of fear in their eyes.

Cortés stared at them steadily. Then he arose, slowly pulled a dagger from his belt and walked toward them. The Aztecs stiffened, expecting death. Instead Cortés walked behind them and cut the binding ropes. He returned to the table and Marina stepped forward to translate for him.

"I regret the inhospitable manner in which these Totonacs have treated you," he said. "We Spaniards do not approve of such things. Our noble king would be grieved if he knew that servants of the great king Montezuma had been so ill-treated in our presence. I want you to return to your king and assure him that the King of Spain and Captain Cortés send their apologies. One of our boats will take you down the coast, well beyond the reach of the Totonacs. Then may you return to Montezuma in safety and comfort, bearing our message."

He made a sign of dismissal and the Aztecs left, following the soldiers.

"Is this the lesson, my captain?" asked Escobar.

"Part of it," said Cortés. "You will learn more in the morning."

The following morning the fat king, supported at each elbow by a courtier, came breathlessly to Cortés' headquarters.

"The prisoners——" he blubbered. "The tax collectors have escaped in the night!"

"What?" Cortés roared. "You great fat fool. What have you done?"

The chief repeated his message, stammering with fright.

"What kind of an ally are you?" asked Cortés, scornfully. "How do you expect our aid when you cannot perform the simplest task or obey the simplest order?"

The fat chief slowly and painfully lowered himself to the ground and placed his forehead on the earth.

"I am your servant, Lord Malinche, and my people are your servants. What you command, we will do."

A few weeks went by. The Spaniards finished building their settlement, which they called Villa

Rica de la Vera Cruz, or "rich town of the true cross."

Cortés called the men together to make a division of the treasures they had thus far obtained. According to the arrangement, one fifth was to go to the king, one fifth to Cortés himself as captain general of the colony, and the remainder was to be divided among the men. But Cortés, anxious to gain favor with the king, laid a different plan before the men.

"Divided, the treasure amounts to but little for each of us," he said, "although altogether it is most impressive. I intend to forgo my share of it, sending it to the king instead. Each of you is entitled to his own share, and that right will be respected. But if all of it is sent to the king it may make an impression that will encourage our future ventures."

Some of the men grumbled, but finally all agreed to give up their shares to the king. The fastest of the sailing vessels was selected, and with old Anton de Alaminos as pilot it set out for Spain with instructions to avoid Cuba, where Diego Velásquez might try to intercept it.

Many of the Spaniards stood on the beach and watched the little ship sail away, wondering when they too might be able to return to the homeland.

Orteguilla, the page, came running to the shore with a message for Cortés.

"Captain," he said, "some Aztecs have come and are awaiting you at your headquarters. Marina says they carry a message from Montezuma."

Cortés hurried back to his headquarters. The

two envoys waited for him with bowed heads. When Cortés had seated himself, one of them spoke.

"Our noble lord Montezuma has sent us to say that he appreciates the generous way in which you treated his tax collectors. The Totonacs will, in time, be punished for their treachery. But since the Totonacs are at present serving you, Lord Montezuma will, out of respect for you, postpone the punishment. He asks us to tell you that your generosity and wisdom have convinced him that you are descendants of the Feathered Serpent god who left us long ago, promising to return. As such you will receive only respect and friendship from the Aztec nation."

The envoys had brought more gifts for the Spaniards, not so many as before but still enough to convince Cortés and his men that they once again were in good standing with Montezuma.

Cortés thanked the Aztecs and assured them that he would soon be paying his respects to Montezuma in person. He also provided a guard to see them safely through the Totonac nation on their way back to Tenochtitlán.

Cortés himself remained seated in his head-quarters. Hands behind his head, he gazed at the cedar beams of the ceiling. Although some of his companions remained with him he spoke as if to himself.

"Our course is now clear. It takes us to Tenochtitlán and its heathen ruler, Montezuma, to gold and power and a new empire for Spain. We must complete the fortification of Villa Rica. And we must prepare for a long, hard march."

XI

SINKING OF THE FLEET

THE LITTLE fortress of Villa Rica, the Spaniards' first settlement in New Spain, was nearly complete.

Cortés took some of the men who had been working on the fortress and led them to the shore of the bay where the ships were anchored. They were to remove everything from the ships, all iron fittings, chains, anchors, ropes, masts, sails—everything that could be removed.

Puzzled, the men went to work and soon had all the rigging piled on the shore.

Cortés then ordered men out in small boats. Each of the ships had a plug in the hull so that the bilge water could be drained out when the ships were careened on a beach. He ordered the plugs pulled in each of them.

The little ships which had brought them to New Spain slowly settled toward the bottom in deep water.

Word of the event reached the settlement of Villa Rica, and soon all the Spaniards were running down to the beach with cries of dismay.

Cortés watched the last of the ships go under water. Then he turned and spoke to his men.

"You are all brave men, but even brave men become confused by things they do not understand. As all of you know, we are to march inland, toward Tenochtitlán. It will be a long march and we know not what lies ahead of us. We may be gone for months, or may be gone for years."

There was a groan at his last words. Cortés went on.

"I have always, and shall always, consider your safety one of my greatest responsibilities. I had examined the hulls of our ships—and remember always that most of them were paid for with gold from my own pocket—and found that they had been dangerously damaged by ship worms. In these waters, worms eat through the wood with great speed. None of the ships was in condition to carry us back to Cuba. In a few more weeks they would have sunk, taking their valuable rigging with them. But with the rigging saved we can, when the time comes, build new hulls."

He paused for a moment. There was some grumbling in the crowd, but no one spoke out, and Cortés continued.

"Tomorrow at dawn we begin our march to the west, a long march and perhaps a dangerous one, taking us into an unknown land. We will leave a garrison here at Villa Rica. The older men and those whose wounds and illnesses have left them unfit to march will remain. And if there are others who do not care for the prospect of this adventure, they too are at liberty to remain if they will only give me their names."

Not a man answered Cortés. The crowd broke up and moved back toward the settlement, and many of the men talked quietly among themselves.

"Does he think we are fools?" asked one. "It is plain he does not fear ship worms so much as he fears the worms of homesickness that gnaw at our minds. Without the ships we are in his hands, whether we will it or no."

"You speak as a child," said another. "You willed yourself into his hands before we left Cuba. You came for gold and adventure and you accepted Hernando Cortés as your leader. If he is a bold and crafty man, do not complain of it but instead be thankful. For only a brave and crafty man can do what we have set out to do."

XII

WESTWARD

THE SPANIARDS were up long before dawn, collecting their gear and checking their weapons. Many of them watched the first red rays of the sun strike the snow-capped mountain peak that they had first seen from their ships. It had become a well-loved sight, and many had learned from Marina the Aztec name for it: Citlaltepetl, or star mountain.

By full daylight the procession had formed and started moving slowly westward.

First there were scouts, moving well ahead of the troops, running quickly and silently to look for ambushes. Then came the horsemen, headed by Cortés himself, all carrying flag-draped lances. They were followed by the main body of Spanish foot soldiers, bearded and ragged but still marching with soldier-like pride. Next came a thousand Totonac porters, naked except for loincloths and staggering under tremendous loads—hampers of food, balls and powder for the cannon, the cannon themselves, boxes of barter goods. Behind the porters marched a smaller group of Spanish soldiers, so placed to make certain that no porters dropped their burdens or disappeared. And finally came a long column of Totonac warriors carrying short spears, bows and arrows and obsidian-edged wooden swords. Their chieftains marched ahead, among the Spanish foot soldiers; where they went the warriors would follow.

It was August, 1519. Cortés and his men had been in New Spain almost half a year.

Their route took them through great tropical forests of giant cedar and mahogany. Many of the trees were hung with orchids, the air was scented with cacao and vanilla. Brilliantly colored birds and butterflies flew around them, and small, shrill-voiced monkeys hid from them among the trees.

As they climbed toward the mountains, the air grew cooler. The Spaniards eagerly sniffed at the aroma of pine forests and shivered in the cold air. Many had copied the quilted cotton armor worn by the Indians, and it afforded them some protection against cold. Others shivered in their steel armor.

They camped for the night, huddling around fires of crackling pine boughs. Cortés, with Marina at his side, spoke with the Totonac chieftains about the route ahead. They could approach Tenochtitlán, he was told, either by way of Cholula, an Aztec holy city, or by way of the republic of Tlascala.

Cholula was a city of worship, with many

temples to the Aztec gods. Its people were not
famed as warriors, but as craftsmen. They were
vassals of Montezuma and were both sly and
treacherous.

Tlascala, although surrounded by Aztec terri-
tory, had managed to remain an independent republic, fighting off the attacks of the Aztecs. The
Tlascalans were great warriors and they were, fur-
thermore, friendly with the Totonacs.

At the urging of the Totonac chieftains Cortés
decided that his army should march by way of
Tlascala.

The route grew more rugged. The little army
filed through wild mountain passes and over great,
boulder-strewn plains between the mountains.
Finally, after nearly two weeks of marching, they
reached the frontier of Tlascala, marked by a great
stone wall made of boulders higher than a man and

many times as thick. Marching along it they came
to an opening and the army filed through.

The land of Tlascala was a high plateau.
Mountains thrust up from the horizon on all sides,
some of them snow-capped; but the plateau itself
was flat, dotted by cultivated fields. Giant maguey
plants, with thick, pointed leaves as high as a
horseman's head, grew in rows. From this plant,
the Spaniards learned, the natives got both a drink,
made of the sap, and fiber for weaving. Here and
there were fields of corn, and there were many
small villages. But all seemed deserted.

The Spaniards were hoping for a warm welcome from the Tlascalans, for an embassy of four
Totonac chieftains had been sent ahead to the city
of Tlascala, carrying gifts and a message that the
Spaniards wished only to pass peacefully through
the country in order to attack their enemies, the
Aztecs. However, as the Spanish soldiers prowled

through the empty villages, they found neither a warm welcome nor food.

Cortés and his horsemen moved on ahead, scouting the strange country. After an hour's riding from the frontier, they came upon a group of thirty Indians dressed for battle, with feathered head-dresses, shields and obsidian-edged swords. Cortés made signs for them to approach, but the Indians turned and ran. Finally the horsemen pursued them. The Indians waited in ambush and suddenly sprang out upon the surprised Spaniards, screaming and slashing with their swords.

The Spanish horsemen fixed their lances and began charging the Indians. They would have made short work of them, but suddenly a much larger force, perhaps of a thousand Indians, came rushing into the battle.

The Tlascalans were fierce fighters and showed no fear of the horses as other Indians had done. Some seized the Spaniards' lances and tried to pull the riders from the saddles. Others attacked the horses, and two of the animals were killed.

All the Spanish horsemen might have been killed if the foot soldiers had not arrived. They set off a volley with muskets and crossbows and the Indian force began to melt away. But they retreated in orderly fashion, taking with them, as trophies, the heads of the two horses they had slain.

As the sound of battle died away, Cortés' men crowded around him, puzzled and angry.

"Why do they attack us, Captain?" they asked. "They were supposed to be friends of the Totonacs, who are our friends, and enemies of the Aztecs. Why is this?"

Cortés shook his head wearily. "That I do not know. I can only guess. If, as we are told, these people have maintained their independence against the Aztecs it may be that they suspect all strangers, fearing them to be in league with the Aztecs."

The Spaniards were disheartened. Many had been wounded and one of the riders died from his wounds. Two of the precious horses had been lost. And worst of all, the Tlascalans, far from being friendly, were the most warlike Indians the Spaniards had yet encountered.

As the Spaniards slowly made their way through the deserted countryside, they met two Tlascalan envoys, accompanied by two of the Totonac chieftains who had been sent ahead. The Tlascalans assured Cortés that the Indian attack had been a mistake. If the Spaniards would proceed to the capital city, they would be received as friends by the Tlascalan ruler.

Since it was growing late, the Spaniards decided to camp for the night in one of the villages. The soldiers searched through the empty houses looking for food. They found a few ears of corn, a few chickens and some fruit covered with sharp thorns but tasting somewhat like figs. And they found a number of strange short-legged, big-bellied little dogs. The Totonac warriors quickly seized the dogs, killed them and prepared to eat them. The Spaniards objected, but the Totonacs explained that the little dogs were raised and fattened for eating, just as were the chickens. Some of the Spaniards were soon roasting dog meat over wood fires; but most of them stretched themselves on the ground, shivering in the cold mountain air, and went to sleep hungry.

Tenochtitlán
(Mexico City)

Chalco

Tlaxcala

Cholula

Route followe
and his army i
MEX

THE FIERCE TLASCALANS

EARLY the next morning the Spaniards resumed their march, taking care to keep their ranks close together in case of a surprise attack. Before they had gone far, they met the two remaining Totonac envoys who had been sent ahead to the Tlascalan capital. Terrified, the Indians told how the Tlascalans had treacherously seized and imprisoned them and thrown Cortés' message and gifts in the fire. Fortunately they had managed to escape during the night, and they brought the unwelcome news that a Tlascalan army was advancing to oppose the Spaniards.

Soon after, the Spaniards came within sight of the enemy. The Tlascalans had massed their forces under red and white banners, and they attacked in never-ending waves, screaming, beating two-tone wooden drums and blowing horns. Arrows and stones fell like rain among the Spaniards. They were forced to fight back to back in order to stay together. The Spaniards finally retreated into a ravine. The Tlascalans, in following them, became a densely packed mass of bodies, and the fire from the Spaniards' muskets and cannon began to take a great toll. Suddenly, at the sound of a horn, the Tlascalans retreated, picking up the bodies of their dead and wounded comrades and carrying them away.

The Spaniards, near exhaustion, climbed to a rocky hilltop crowned by a sort of temple or tower. Almost all the men and horses had suffered wounds. The men dropped to the ground, treated their wounds as best they could, tightened crossbow strings and tried to make themselves ready for another battle. Fortunately they found a plentiful supply of food in some neighboring huts.

The hilltop was turned into a fortified camp. Cortés divided his men into four equal groups and alternated them on watch duty. Those who were not on guard slept fully dressed for battle, swords in their hands, and the horses were kept saddled and bridled at all times. Most of the Spaniards had suffered from fever, and here in the highlands they were afflicted with chills. Cortés himself could, at times, hardly sit in his saddle.

The Spaniards had taken a few prisoners. The next day Cortés released them, asking them to repeat to their chieftains his earlier message: that the Spaniards meant no harm and wished only peaceful passage through the republic of Tlascala.

Back came a message from the Indians: "Proceed to our capital. There we will make peace with you by eating your flesh and we will pay tribute to our gods with your hearts and blood." The Tlascalans were reported to have formed an army of 50,000 men.

The Spaniards groaned at the news. All through the night the priests heard confessions from exhausted soldiers who were convinced they would never live through another day.

Nevertheless the Spaniards were ready for battle the next morning. Cortés gave orders: the crossbowmen must use their darts sparingly—half of them should be loading while the others shot; the musketeers must do the same; the swordsmen must thrust at the Indians' stomachs to keep them at a distance; the lancers were to thrust at their faces and keep the lances from their grasp.

The Spaniards limped out to meet the Tlascalan army. They found them, scarcely a mile from their own camp. The Indians attacked immediately, hurling fire-hardened wooden spears until the ground was covered and the Spaniards had difficulty walking over them. The Indians rushed forward, closely packed and screaming. The cannon roared, and the first wave of Indians faltered and stopped. But a second wave came on. The musketeers and crossbowmen began shooting steadily into the mass of bronze bodies.

Although the Tlascalans were more numerous than before, they had learned to fear both the gunfire and the horsemen. Groups of them began to withdraw from the field, dragging their dead and wounded with them. Finally all retreated. The Spaniards, too fatigued to pursue them, returned to their hilltop fortress. After treating their wounds

they dug graves for those of their own number who had been killed, carefully covering the graves with stones so that the Tlascalans would not dig them up and discover that Spaniards, like Tlascalans, were ordinary, mortal men.

While the Spaniards were doing this, the Tlascalans were holding a council of war. They called in their priests and wise men for advice. Why, the warriors wanted to know, could not a large and powerful Tlascalan army defeat this little army of strangers? There were a hundred Tlascalans for every Spaniard. Were the white men gods?

The priests, after discussing the matter, answered: The white men were not gods. But they were descendants of the sun god. They received their power from the sun. If attacked after sundown they would be helpless.

So the bravest and ablest of the Tlascalan chieftains took 10,000 of their best fighters and stealthily approached the Spanish camp in the night.

But the Spaniards, weary though they were, could not be surprised. When a sentry gave the alarm they sprang from the ground, fully armed and armored, and charged the Indians in the moonlight. The Indians, shocked by the mistake their priests had made, quickly retreated and the Spanish horsemen pursued them across the moonlit plain.

Cortés slowly led the horsemen back to camp. His face was yellow in the moonlight and his body shook with chills.

"Captain, Captain," said one of his companions, "will this never end? We have lost forty-five men in this wretched place, more than one-tenth our total strength—except for our Indian allies, and I do not put much store in them. Our faith, our arms and our valor have beaten off each attack, but there is ever another attack. We have won our battles, but another such victory we cannot afford."

"We shall try, once more, to persuade them," said Cortés, his teeth chattering with a fever chill.

Again he sent captured prisoners as messengers to the Tlascalans, repeating the message he had sent before.

This time the Tlascalans were ready for peace. They sent porters with supplies of food for the

WORLD
Landmark
BOOKS

W-45

CAPTAIN
Cortés
CONQUERS
Mexico

by William Johnson

starving Spaniards. The porters were followed by the nation's chieftains. They made signs of peace. They had fought, they said, because they feared Cortés and his men were in league with Montezuma, who had always sought to defeat them by treachery. They invited the Spaniards to come with them to their capital, live with them and be friends.

THE CHANGING MIND

THE TLASCALANS were not the only ones to have a change of heart regarding the Spaniards.

So had Montezuma.

As usual, his spies had reported everything to him. The Aztec ruler listened in amazement to the way in which a few Spaniards, ill, hungry and wounded, had defeated the fierce Tlascalans whom the Aztecs, in a hundred years of battle, had been unable to vanquish.

He was even more alarmed when he realized that his old enemies, the Tlascalans, would now become the allies of these strange white men from the east. He sent new emissaries to visit Cortés.

Cortés and his men were preparing to break camp and move on to the Tlascalan capital when the mission from Montezuma arrived. The five Aztecs were tall, haughty and richly dressed. They approached Cortés ceremoniously, waving pots of incense and unwrapping new gifts of gold and cloth.

Montezuma, they said, was overjoyed by the Spaniards' victory over the Tlascalans. He was so impressed with the Spaniards' valor and behavior that he would gladly become a vassal of their king across the sea. He would pay, each year, a tribute of gold.

Excellent, said Cortés.

But there was one condition that must be met before Montezuma would accept the foreign king as his superior, said the Aztecs.

And what, asked Cortés, was that condition?

"That you, Lord Malinche, and your men and your Totonac allies, come no farther; that you return to the shores of the sea and come no closer to Tenochtitlán."

Cortés had, at first, smiled. Now he scowled at the Aztecs and replied:

"Tell Lord Montezuma that we are delighted by his decision to accept our king as his. But tell him also that we still intend to visit him in his capital, though we will remain for a time with our friends, the Tlascalans."

The Aztecs bowed again and withdrew, and the Spaniards went on with their move to Tlascala, a mountain city which still exists.

The Tlascalans, fierce in warfare, now did everything to make the Spaniards comfortable. A large building with an open courtyard was assigned to them. The Spaniards cleaned themselves in the public baths and put on shirts made for them by Tlascalan women from the cloth that had come from Montezuma. They slept on straw pallets and ate the best food the Tlascalans could provide.

Surrounded as they were by the Aztecs, there were many things the Tlascalans did not possess, such as salt and cacao. On the other hand they had abundant supplies of corn, and gradually the Spaniards recovered their strength.

The Aztec emissaries came once more to call on Cortés. The Spanish captain, taking his interpreters with him, shut himself in a room with them. The Spanish soldiers clustered outside the room. Finally the emissaries came out, followed by Cortés. The Aztecs bowed low and walked away. All the soldiers looked closely at Cortés.

"What did they say?" someone shouted.

Cortés smiled at his men and waited for them to be quiet.

"Our friend, Lord Montezuma, has changed his mind again. He now agrees that he will welcome us into his city."

"And why has he changed his mind?" someone asked.

"It is plain," said Cortés, "that he fears our friendship with the Tlascalans."

"And when do we march on Tenochtitlán?"

"Tomorrow. But we do not go there directly. We will march, instead, by way of the city of Cholula. It is another approach to Tenochtitlán."

The men cheered. After a week's rest they were ready to go again. At dawn the next day they lined up in marching order. Six thousand Tlascalan warriors joined them. The Tlascalan chieftains wanted to send many times that number, but Cortés restrained them.

"We do not want to appear to be on our way to war," explained Cortés.

The little army marched southward along a straight, tree-lined path. A day's march brought them to the outskirts of Cholula. The city's skyline was dotted with pyramid-temples shining in the evening sun. Cholula was a holy city, noted for its temples. Similarly, Cholula today is noted for its many churches.

A delegation of Cholulan chieftains came out to meet the Spaniards. Quarters and food had been prepared for them within the city, they said. Cortés might bring his own men and his Totonac allies into the city, but the Tlascalans must remain outside; they were ancient enemies and the Cholulans did not trust them.

The Tlascalans camped at the side of the road while the Spaniards and the Totonacs marched into the city. The road was lined with men, women and children, all dressed in long cotton robes more richly decorated than any the Spaniards had yet seen.

Again the army was quartered in a courtyard, and Cholulan women brought supplies of food— fowl, ground corn, vegetables and fruit. There was a strange red fruit that the Spaniards came later to know as the tomato, and there were fiery-flavored red and green peppers.

Late the next day the Aztec emissaries once more arrived at the Spaniards' quarters. They were taken to Cortés, for whom they had an important message. Montezuma had sent word that, much as he regretted it, Tenochtitlán, his capital, was short of food. It would therefore be better if they did not come.

Cortés' face flushed with anger.

"What kind of a ruler is this who cannot make up his mind—an invitation one day, a rejection the next?" He paused, staring angrily at his visitors.

"No, Marina," he said to his interpreter, "do not tell them that. Tell them instead that our plans have advanced too far for changing, that we will march on Tenochtitlán on the day after tomorrow and that we shall expect treatment that one noble king should extend to the emissaries of another." The Aztec messengers frowned as they heard this, and left, sullenly.

There then began a series of events which alarmed the Spaniards.

First, word came from the Tlascalans who were camped outside the city that there were 20,000 Aztec warriors hiding in the hills outside of Cholula, apparently preparing to ambush the Spaniards.

Next, a Totonac scout reported that deep pits had been dug in some of the streets of Cholula. In the pits there were sharpened poles, and the pits were covered with brush, apparently as traps for the Spaniards' horses.

Another scout reported that great cooking pots with supplies of tomatoes and peppers had been taken to the largest pyramids in preparation for a sacrifice and a feast on human flesh.

And Marina brought to Cortés a Cholulan woman, the wife of a priest. "She wanted me to go home with her, master," she told Cortés, "so that I would be safe when the attack comes."

During the night the Spaniards could hear the sound of drums beating and could see great fires blazing on the tops of the pyramids.

The next morning, at the hour when food should have been brought, there was no food.

Cortés called some of his leaders into conference. After discussing the ominous developments, he called the Cholulan chieftains before him.

"Tomorrow," he told them, "shortly after dawn, we will leave your city, marching toward Tenochtitlán where we will be guests of the great Montezuma. As subjects of Montezuma you will be expected to aid us. Before our departure, you will bring us ample supplies for our journey. We will also expect all chieftains and principal men to be here to bid us farewell; thus we can report to the Lord Montezuma that you have treated us in friendly and courteous fashion."

The Spanish soldiers were then given instructions, and messengers were sent to the camp of the Tlascalan allies.

That night the Spaniards rested uneasily. Few slept, and within the courtyard many whispered among themselves and listened to the frightening sound of drums.

Before dawn they were up and ready. They took posts around the courtyard, and heavy guards were stationed at the gates. The Cholulans arrived, first the chieftains, dressed in long cotton mantles and wearing waving plumes on their heads; then came a thousand or more warriors and hundreds of porters carrying the requested supplies. They were directed into the center of the courtyard and the Spaniards massed themselves around the gates so that no one could leave.

Cortés, mounted on his horse and armed for battle, addressed the chieftains.

"We came among you peacefully," he said, his face stern. "We had been informed by the great Montezuma, your lord, that you would receive us in friendly fashion.

"But instead you have met us with treachery. We know of the warriors you have ready to attack us. We know of the traps you have dug for our horses. We know of your plans to sacrifice us on your blood-stained pyramids.

"Our noble king from across the sea repays loyalty and friendship with kindness, love and protection. But treachery he treats only with punishment and death!"

With the word "death" Cortés raised his sword. Musket fire rattled from all sides and the cannon roared. The Cholulans, close-packed in the center of the courtyard, screamed with fear and pain. The Spaniards charged among them, chopping with their swords and thrusting with their lances. In minutes the Indian bodies were piled high. Outside, the Tlascalans, who had secretly crept into the city before dawn, ran through the streets, screaming and killing and throwing lighted torches into the buildings.

Within an hour Cholula, by far the handsomest city the Spaniards had thus far found in the new world, was a ruin.

Cortés stood on the courtyard wall and looked out over the smoking city. His face was sad. Escobar stood beside him.

"I do not understand it, my captain," said Escobar.

"Understand what, my son?"

"If they were really going to attack us, surely

they would have done it during the night, knowing that we planned to leave in the morning. Or, if they did not do that, then why would they come peacefully and unarmed to our quarters, as you ordered. Why did they not attack instead? Or was there really a plot?"

"We had good reason to suspect a plot," said Cortés. "And in warfare the faintest suspicion calls for action, heartless though the action may be. I am saddened, as you are, by this sight, but we had no alternative.

"But all this death and destruction may bring some good. Word of it will get to Montezuma. He will see how we Spaniards react to treachery. It will give him something to consider if he has, perhaps, thought of some trap for us in Tenochtitlán."

CONFLICT OF THE GODS

BEFORE THE massacre at Cholula was over, spies for Montezuma were speeding westward toward their capital. Before sundown the news was brought to the Aztec ruler. He listened gloomily while the spies described the scene.

When they finished speaking he arose, left his palace and walked slowly across a wide plaza. All activity in the plaza ceased; his subjects stood still with downcast eyes. He approached the great pyramid that stood at one side of the plaza, and two black-robed priests fell into step with him, one on either side. Slowly climbing the steep stone steps to the summit, he looked out over his city, now growing dark in the evening shade. To the southeast the peaks of the two snow-capped volcanoes, Popocatépetl and Ixtaccíhuatl, reflected the yellow hues of the setting sun. Beyond the volcanoes lay Cholula, where the strange white men and their small army had just committed an outrage against his subjects.

There was a wooden shrine atop the pyramid. Montezuma walked into the shrine and stopped before an idol. The figure, many times as large as a man, had a cruel, snarling face, and around his body coiled a snake made of pearls and precious stones. One hand held a bow; the other, a bunch of golden arrows. Around one ankle was a garland of hummingbird feathers.

"Oh, Hummingbird Wizard," said Montezuma, speaking softly. "Oh, fearsome war god, I come as always to offer my devotion. But the problems that beset my people are not the problems of war. I must go to ask the help of your brother god, he of the Smoking Mirror."

Walking backward, Montezuma left the shrine.

He descended from the pyramid and crossed the great plaza to another sanctuary. This was the shrine of the Smoking Mirror god who, the Aztecs believed, had created the world and was responsible for its well being. The idol was simpler and less fearsome than that of the war god. The figure was of polished black stone, adorned with plates of gold and strings of precious stones. On one arm was a dark mirror in which the god was thought to be able to see coming events.

In front of the idol was a sacrificial stone, a huge block on which the priests stretched their victims before plunging stone knives into their chests. At one side of the idol a fire of sweet-smelling pine knots burned in a brazier; at the other side was a golden dish containing human hearts left from the morning's sacrifice.

Montezuma bowed low, then arose, went forward, took one of the hearts and threw it in the fire. A cloud of dense, evil-smelling smoke arose.

"Direct me, wise and all-knowing one," said Montezuma and continued to stand, staring into the black face of the idol.

When it was quite dark he left the shrine. The two priests followed him at a distance as he slowly returned to his palace.

Somewhat later six of his principal warriors were summoned into the ruler's presence. Each of them wore full battle dress. Montezuma sat cross-legged on an animal skin. He was caressing a tame

jaguar, holding it by a golden chain and feeding it pieces of meat from a glowing brazier. After a long silence he spoke.

"Again we must change our plans. These white strangers do things that only the gods can understand. In Cholula they read our minds and knew what it was that we had planned for them. It seems plain that they are the children of the Feathered Serpent god. They could not do these things as men, but only as gods or godlike men.

"We are men, not gods. If this is a conflict between our gods whom we have venerated, and the Feathered Serpent god, whom we have neglected, then we are helpless. We shall continue to revere the Smoking Mirror and the Hummingbird Wizard. But we must not offend the Feathered Serpent. If these are his children we must welcome them among us and make them comfortable and listen to what they have to say to us.

"You will call in the army that is lying in ambush for them at Cholula, and you will prepare the city to welcome the strangers."

One of the warriors, his face troubled, was about to speak, but Montezuma silenced him with an upraised hand. All of them bowed low and withdrew. It became silent in the palace. The jaguar slept and Montezuma gazed at the dying coals in the brazier.

THE SMOKING MOUNTAIN

THE SPANIARDS did not leave Cholula immediately, but spent ten more days there trying to restore some order to the wrecked city. They installed a new chieftain who was friendly to them and who could, Cortés felt, be trusted. The thousands of bodies were collected and burned on great funeral pyres. The Spaniards broke open the wooden-barred cages in which the Cholulans had kept prisoners intended for sacrifice, and set them free. They took possession of the largest of the many pyramids in the city, destroyed the idols that had been there and erected a huge stone cross, the symbol of their own religion.

The Totonac warriors were allowed to return to their homeland, and Cortés permitted the Tlascalans to arm and equip themselves with weapons and clothing seized from the defeated Cholulans. In new quilted cotton armor and carrying stout

wooden shields and obsidian-edged swords, the Tlascalans made an impressive army.

Finally Cortés gave the order to march, and
the long procession filed north and west to the
pass between the two volcanoes. Their route rose
higher and higher and the air grew colder. Finally
the clouds swirled around the marching column
and Cortés called a halt. Popocatépetl, or "the
smoking mountain," was on their left, and Ixtaccíhuatl, or "the sleeping princess," on their right.
In the mythology of the region, the smoking mountain was an Aztec warrior who stood guard over
the sleeping princess.

Diego de Ordaz asked if he might climb Popocatépetl. Cortés granted permission, for he wanted
to rest his troops and porters after the ascent they
had already made. Ordaz took Escobar and eight
other Spanish soldiers with him, all volunteers, plus
a group of Tlascalan warriors.

The route was steep and dangerous, leading
first through a dense forest, then over a track of
black volcanic ash and lava that had been thrown
out during eruptions. When they reached an area
of great, jagged rocks, the Tlascalans turned back,
saying in sign language that to go farther would
anger the gods of the mountain.

The Spaniards kept on, laboring harder as the
ascent grew steeper and the air thinner. Then they
came to snow and ice, and far above them they
could see the cratered peak with smoke rising from
it. Occasionally there would be a rumble under
the earth and great puffs of smoke and steam
would rise from the crater. As the wind shifted,
clouds of gas and showers of ashes were swept

down on the struggling mountain climbers. Finally Ordaz called a halt. The men sat for a few minutes on an icy ledge to rest, then wearily got to their feet and started the dangerous descent. Passing ice caves they broke off huge icicles to take to their companions below.

When they reached the pass where the troops were halted, Ordaz presented the largest icicle to Cortés. Then the column moved on again.

Icy winds swept down from the mountains, buffeting the men with sleet and snow. As night fell they reached a large stone building. This was one of the shelters the Aztecs had built to accommodate the messengers and carriers who went to and fro constantly, carrying orders of the Aztec monarch out to his faraway subjects, bringing back information, or carrying loads of fresh fruits from the tropics and fish from the sea. The Spaniards crowded into the building and, protected from the whistling mountain winds, spent a comfortable night.

The next day they continued the descent into the great valley of Mexico. At times the route carried them through great forests; at other times they crossed high ridges. As the Spaniards rounded a corner on the crest of the sierra of Ahualco, the clouds lifted and there, far below, stood the great city of Tenochtitlán, surrounded by water. The water reflected the blue of the sky and the floating clouds so that the city appeared to be floating in mid-air.

The men gasped, staring in silence. They could see the three great causeways leading to the mainland and the many pyramids of the city with smoke rising from them.

The Spaniards had learned to associate pyramids with human sacrifice. Now they wondered if they ever could conquer such a city. Or would they end their lives as captive sacrifices on the pyramids?

Cortés sensed their uneasiness. He halted the column and spoke to them.

"Before us lies the capital of New Spain. With luck, it will one day be the greatest city of Spain, and we will be remembered as the men who brought this great prize as a gift to our mother country. Tomorrow we will be in the city as honored guests of the great Montezuma. At least so he indicated in his latest communication. We will be permitted to enter unharmed and will be treated as guests. But Montezuma is a changeable man. We must be prepared for his changes of mind, ready at all times to fight for our lives and the glory of God and our noble king. We must constantly exercise an iron discipline. If you are not prepared to give me complete and unquestioning obedience we will halt at this point and you may choose a leader to whom you can give such obedience."

There were shouts of "No! No!"

Cortés smiled and gave the command to proceed.

MONTEZUMA

AS THE Spanish army moved down out of the mountains and into the valley, they passed through many villages. The villagers were curious and friendly. They stared in amazement at the horses, pointed at the Spaniards' white faces, and brought gifts of flowers and fruits.

Finally the marching column came to the water's edge and moved out on one of the great stone causeways leading to Tenochtitlán. It was wide enough for four horsemen to ride abreast. Indians skimmed over the surface of the lake in canoes, some busily paddling loads of vegetables and chickens toward the capital, others merely idling, coming close to the causeway to stare at the strangers.

The Spaniards marched with their eyes straight ahead, staring at the city. It was even larger than they had thought. The buildings were built of

stone. Most of them had flat roofs on which flowers
grew in profusion. At regular intervals canals entered the city, and in and out of them flowed a
heavy traffic of canoes.

The causeway ended in a broad avenue that
appeared to go into the heart of the city. As the
Spaniards approached the end of the causeway,
they could see a procession coming out the avenue,
moving slowly toward them. Cortés called a halt
and his men waited for the procession to reach
them, wondering once more if they were going to
be welcomed or betrayed.

First came three Aztecs carrying heavily orna-
mented golden pikes; from the middle pike floated
a flag with an eagle embroidered upon it. Back of
them marched a large body of richly dressed warriors carrying on their shoulders a golden litter,
decorated with a tapestry of feather work in red,
blue and green and draped with strings of jewels
and silver tassels. The litter bearers halted a short
distance in front of the Spaniards and carefully
lowered their burden. Two of them unrolled a
snowy white cloth on the stone pavement of the
causeway, and the occupant of the litter stepped
out. He was taller than his companions and his
skin was somewhat lighter in color. His face was
thin and handsome and he bore himself with great
dignity. His robe, which fell to his ankles, was
white embroidered with gold. He wore a headdress
of waving green plumes and his sandals were of
gold. His companions threw themselves to the
ground as he walked slowly towards the Spaniards.

"It is the Lord Montezuma," said Marina.

Cortés dismounted, handed his reins to Escobar, and walked forward to meet Montezuma. He bowed gravely. Speaking through Marina, he thanked Montezuma for the many gifts he had sent and said that the Aztecs' generosity was appreciated by the Spanish king who was his lord.

"It is nothing," Montezuma replied. "We are proud to welcome you to our city. Such riches as we possess we gladly share with your noble lord."

The Spaniards standing back of Cortés nudged one another and grinned.

"My brother," said Montezuma, summoning one of the nobles who accompanied him, "will guide you through the city and to the quarters we have prepared for you in the palace of my father. May your stay among us be filled with peace and contentment."

Cortés took from his throat a necklace of glass beads and placed it around Montezuma's neck. Then, in the Spanish manner, he started to give Montezuma an embrace as a gesture of friendship.

The Aztec warriors jumped forward, scowling fiercely, and thrust Cortés back.

"You must not touch the person of the king," said Marina.

Cortés bowed his head and Montezuma returned to his litter. Cortés remounted his horse and the Spaniards moved forward, following the Aztec noble whom Montezuma had given them as a

guide. As the column moved slowly into the city, the Spaniards exclaimed in amazement at the grandeur of the buildings made with red stone and white stucco. They passed busy markets where thousands of people gathered to buy from vendors; stately buildings with great flower gardens; ordinary houses of wood and thatch; public houses from which came weird music of flutes and drums.

Cortés turned to his chamberlain: "What do you make of this, Escobar? When we met on the quay at Santiago had you ever dreamed of such sights as we now see?"

"No, my captain. It is beautiful and grand and exciting and makes me want to throw my cap in the air. The music is not like our music, but I like it."

Cortés pointed ahead. A huge pyramid loomed above the flat-roofed buildings, smoke rising from its peak.

"It is well to admire their arts, their fine buildings, their wealth and their music. But it is also well to remember the pyramids, where they make sacrifices to their heathen idols. The body of some unfortunate soul makes the smoke we now see. If we have been alert in the past, now we must be more so for we are in their midst. We have always been steadfast in our faith but now we must be more so because we are surrounded by symbols of the devil. And always we must be as brave and daring as only Spaniards can be."

HIDDEN TREASURE

THE PROCESSION carrying Montezuma turned and entered a great palace on the right. The Spaniards, following their guide, moved on. Beyond Montezuma's house stood a temple; from the summit wild-eyed priests looked down upon them.

"The temple of the Smoking Mirror god," Marina explained.

Beyond the temple was an aviary, a stone building surmounted by great wooden cages in which birds of many sizes and colors fluttered and sang. And beyond it lay the palace of Axayacatl, Montezuma's father. This was to be the Spaniards' quarters. The marchers moved through a wide gate and into a great paved courtyard. The palace extended around it on all sides.

The horses, equipment and the Tlascalan allies were left in the courtyard and the Spaniards were shown to rooms in the palace. For each there was a bed of straw mats covered with fine cotton cloth.

Cortés was given the largest apartment of the palace, looking out over the great plaza. His pages, Orteguilla and Salazar, his chamberlain, Escobar, his interpreters, Aguilar and Marina, shared the apartment with him.

Escobar and the pages, as soon as they had attended to their duties, stood at one of the embrasures looking out on the plaza. Before them, in the center of the plaza, stood the largest pyramid of all, rising in four tiers. At its summit were two small wooden shrines; smoke continued to pour out of them.

At one side of the pyramid was a great building constructed like a cage; it was filled to the top with human skulls.

Here and there were paved streets, but the rest of the city was divided only by canals on which canoes floated. Beyond the great pyramid was a basin in which many of the canoes were moored.

The three Spanish youths heard Cortés call them and ran back to their duties. Montezuma was coming to pay a visit.

Cortés and the other Spaniards stood at attention as the Aztec king approached. He had changed his robe for one of blue and white, and the attendants who followed him wore gowns of green. Two of them walked at Montezuma's side, holding his arms as though to support him, although he obviously needed no support since he stood erect and walked with a firm step; the others carried bunches of flowers and bowls of incense, which they swung to and fro.

Porters followed them with leather cases full of

gifts—more intricately contrived golden ornaments and cloaks of woven feathers. Montezuma himself presented a gift to Cortés: a necklace made of tiny golden shrimps.

"Malinche," said Montezuma, "forgive me if in the past we have seemed unfriendly and inhospitable. But we have had much to study, determining our proper course. Since the first white man from the east came to our shores—and there were two groups that came before you and your men—we have studied your ways, your methods of fighting and living and praying to the god of the wooden cross. You have been watched closely and everything you have done has been reported to me.

"I am a warrior, but I am also a student of our religion. I have consulted with our priests, have considered various omens and have studied the history of our people engraved on the stone walls of our temples. It is now clear that you are descended from the white god who once ruled this land, before my people came. Therefore you are welcome in our land, Malinche."

Cortés nodded gravely when Montezuma's words had been translated for him.

He made a speech of appreciation, mentioned his own king and his own land, and said that he would like to ask two things.

"Ask what you will," replied Montezuma.

"First," said Cortés, "I should like permission to build a chapel in this palace which you have placed at our disposal so that my men and I can worship our own God in our own way."

"Please do as you will," said Montezuma. "I shall order workmen, our finest artisans, to come with building materials, stone and timber. You have only to direct them."

"And I should like," said Cortés, "to return the courtesy of this visit by coming to see you in your own palace and by going with you to your places of worship."

"Come then," said Montezuma. "I will await you in my palace."

Cortés selected a few of his leaders to accompany him. They cleaned themselves and their clothing as best they could. Cortés wrapped himself in his now dingy black velvet cloak, put on a plumed hat and led them toward Montezuma's palace.

The palace was a great, one-story building built of the porous red stone which was common in the city. The roof was of elaborately carved cedar beams. Over the entrance was a marble slab with Montezuma's coat of arms: an eagle with an ocelot clutched in his talons.

Inside, the air was fragrant with incense, and through openings the Spaniards could see great gardens with huge trees, beds of strange flowers and fountains sparkling in the sun. The walls were covered with tapestries, worked in designs of strange animals and monsters, and the stone floors were covered with palm-leaf mats.

"Don Carlos, our noble king, lives no more grandly than this heathen monarch," said Cortés; and his followers, their faces blank with amazement at what they saw, nodded.

Finally, after passing through many corridors, they were led into the great apartment that was Montezuma's reception room. Montezuma sat cross-legged on a low wooden platform. He bade the

Spaniards to seat themselves on the fur rugs that covered the floor before him. Women servants placed in front of each of them a golden cup filled with a thick, reddish brown liquid that had been stirred to a froth. It was *chocolatl,* the Aztec drink, made from cacao beans which the Aztecs also used for money. Flavored with vanilla and other spices, it was rich and refreshing.

Trays of food were passed to the Spaniards: chunks of roast meat, ears of green Indian corn, or maize, that had been cooked in the husk, and bowls of bright fruit that Aztec runners had brought only that morning from the tropics.

The Spaniards ate and drank hungrily. Montezuma ate little but regularly took sips from his golden cup of chocolatl. His elderly counselors stood at one side. Now and then Montezuma would hold out a bit of food to one of them. The man would bow low, take the food from his emperor's hand, and walk slowly backward with head bowed until he was at a proper distance for eating.

"He feeds his people as we feed our dogs," whispered Pedro de Alvarado.

"Be quiet," said Cortés.

When Montezuma had finished he rinsed his hands in a silver bowl of perfumed water, and the Spaniards did the same in the bowls that were placed beside them.

Then Montezuma clapped his hands and two dwarfs ran into the room. One was hunchbacked and the other had short legs that were grotesquely bowed. They wore costumes of many colors decorated with rows of silver shells which tinkled as they moved. The dwarfs bowed before Montezuma and then to the Spaniards and began tumbling,

turning somersaults, juggling golden balls and balancing feathers on their noses.

When Montezuma raised his hand the clowns left and the Spaniards prepared to return to their own quarters. Montezuma said that he would come for them the next day and take them to the pyramid.

Cortés and his companions, when they returned to their own palace, found their followers in a great state of excitement.

"You must come see what we have found, my captain," said one. "You will hardly believe it."

Cortés followed the man through the palace and down an incline to an underground room.

"We were cleaning this room to make it our

chapel," the man explained. "And here," pointing to a great hole in the wall, "we found a place where the plaster was fresh. We chipped it away, removed the stones and found another room. Follow me."

Cortés followed the man through the hole. Inside, Spanish soldiers held aloft pine torches which cast a smoky light in the dark room. The walls of the room were carved with the forms of serpents which seemed to writhe and move in the flickering, uncertain light.

And on the floor, in careless piles, were stacked more gold and silver than the Spaniards had ever seen—ornaments, plates, vases, helmets, boxes of pearls and jade.

Cortés squatted on the floor and examined the treasure.

"Now," he said, "we are beginning to find that which we sought, the thing that made us leave our homes and families to face the dreadful dangers and discomforts of a heathen land. If there is this much here, hidden away and forgotten, think how much more there must be in the palace of Montezuma himself. Let us close the room. Replace the stones and plaster so that no one will know we have been here. The treasure will wait while we find more to go with it."

XIX

THE PYRAMID

GUIDED BY Montezuma himself, Cortés and his principal officers toured the city of Tenochtitlán.

They visited market places larger and more crowded than any they remembered in Spain. Here they saw vast supplies of strange food, mounds of grain and fruit, piles of bright-colored peppers, fish, carcasses of wild animals, chickens, ducks and the strange little dogs these people raised for food. There were arrows, spears, gaily decorated shields, wooden swords with obsidian edges, helmets made to resemble the heads of animals and birds. There were piles of the cacao beans that the Aztecs used as money, stacks of earthen pottery, little piles of gold dust and boxes of jewelry, necklaces of gold and silver and ear plugs made of jade, mother of pearl and precious stones. Here a woman carefully plucked small feathers from a parrot and wove them into a feather tapestry. Another woman near by took ground corn, mixed it with water and slapped it between her palms until it was thin as paper, after which she baked it over coals and offered it for sale. A hunter displayed the skins of wild animals, and on a raised stone platform a merchant had slaves to sell.

From the market place they went on to the great pyramid near the Spanish quarters. It was built like four boxes with sloping sides, placed one atop another, each smaller than the last. They ascended by climbing the first one, walking a broad ledge to the other side and ascending another stairway.

At the top Montezuma led them to the edge and swept his arm in a broad circle. "This is our city, Malinche."

The Spaniards could see the entire city with its network of canals and the surrounding lake, the three causeways leading from the island city to the villages and towns beyond, and the ranges of mountains beyond them.

Below, in the plaza, were several smaller temples and the great wooden crib filled with human skulls. Near it was an enclosure in which great quantities of weapons, lances, bows, swords and shields were stored.

Montezuma led them to the temple that stood on the flat, stone top of the pyramid. Within the temple were two shrines. On one stood the huge idol of the Hummingbird Wizard, the Aztecs' war god. The Spaniards stared at the hideous, piercing eyes and the great body encircled with snakes, and shuddered. Before the idol was a sacrificial stone; this stone, as well as the floors and walls around

it, was encrusted with blood. The other shrine was
dedicated to the Smoking Mirror god. Though he
was a milder deity, there was blood on his altar
too, giving evidence of more human sacrifice. Several of the Spaniards excused themselves to get out
into the fresh air. Cortés' face was pale, but he
stayed at Montezuma's side.

"Lord Montezuma," Cortés said, "you are a
wise man and should know that these idols are
false gods and devils. Will you allow us to erect
the cross of our religion here on your pyramid? It
is the sign of the true religion and it will in time
show you the falseness of these wicked devils."

Montezuma's eyes widened and he stared at
Cortés in disbelief. Some of the Spaniards wondered if their leader had gone too far.

"Malinche," said Montezuma, speaking slowly
and very distinctly, "you desecrate our gods, the
gods of our fathers who have led us to victory in
war and have made the rains to come, the fields
fertile and the seeds to sprout. This we cannot
bear; you must go now."

Cortés followed Montezuma out of the shrine
and toward the edge of the pyramid. He stopped
by a wooden drum as broad as a wagon wheel
and almost the height of a man. Its sides were
carved to resemble a great, coiled snake.

"One more question, Lord Montezuma. What
is this?"

Montezuma regarded Cortés haughtily.

"It is our signal drum," he said. "It is used
to call our people for festivals of worship." He
nodded at a priest. The priest seized a wooden
stick on the end of which a human skull was

mounted. Standing on a platform he swung the
stick high over his head and struck the surface.
There was a hollow boom. The sound floated out
over the city and the Spaniards could see the people, far below, stop and look toward the pyramid.

"It also calls them to war," said Montezuma,
and started down the face of the pyramid. The
Spaniards followed him slowly and thoughtfully.

XX

CAPTIVE KING

A WEEK went by. The Spaniards, accustomed to activity, were growing restless. Food was brought to them each day. When they were not eating they slept or did nothing. Cortés had ordered them not to leave the palace, fearing some incident.

Finally Cortés called some of his leaders to a meeting—Pedro de Alvarado, Juan Velásquez de Leon, Diego de Ordaz and Gonzalo de Sandoval. Sandoval was younger than the rest, a slender young man who showed much promise and reliability.

"We are in an impossible situation," said Cortés. "We are in the heart of this heathen nation. They have accepted us as guests, not as conquerors, because the heathen superstitions of their king have led him to believe this is the thing to do.

"His superstitions can change. With one beat of that great drum on the pyramid he could call his people into war against us. Here we would be trapped. We have no boats to cross the lake, and the causeways are broken by drawbridges. They could open those and have us trapped. Our hearts and our blood would join those we saw on the great pyramid."

"What can we do?" someone asked.

"We will make the great Montezuma a captive, here in our own quarters, as a hostage for our safety."

"How?"

"We will persuade him to come of his own will. We will go to his palace now to arrange it. You four will accompany me. Escobar, you and Orteguilla will go ahead with Marina to tell Montezuma of our coming."

Montezuma had forgotten the insults to his gods and welcomed the Spaniards warmly, ordering chocolate to be served.

Cortés ignored the chocolate.

"Lord Montezuma," he said, "word has come to me, from the garrison we left at Villa Rica, that your vassals in that area have been guilty of great treachery against our brother soldiers. First they slew two of our men who had gone to them on a peaceful mission. When our garrison called them to account, they battled us and killed eight more of our soldiers."

The other Spaniards stared at Cortés with surprise. They had not heard this news before. Cortés had received the report while they were still in Cholula and had not told them. Escobar, listening to his captain, wondered why he had not made a complaint when they first met Montezuma. Perhaps this was more of the captain's diplomacy.

Montezuma protested that he knew nothing of the event. "What can I do, Malinche?"

"They are your vassals," said Cortés. "They do nothing without your command. What they have done, then, is your responsibility."

"But Malinche, I assure you I knew nothing of it. In a realm as vast as mine a king cannot know everything. What can I do to make amends for the loss of your brothers?"

"You must send for this vassal chieftain who was guilty of the treachery, so that he may be punished," said Cortés.

Montezuma detached from his wrist a pendant carved in jade. Calling one of his courtiers to his side, he handed him the pendant and gave him instructions. The courtier hurried away.

"When Quauhpopoca sees the amulet he will come at once," said Montezuma. "I hope that this will satisfy you, Malinche, and calm your grief. I will see that justice is done and you will see that I am innocent in the matter."

"Very well," said Cortés, "but we must have assurance of this."

"You have my word, Malinche."

"We need more. We want you to come and stay with us in our quarters until this matter is settled."

Montezuma stared at him, his mouth open. "I could not do that; I would be your prisoner."

"No, not our prisoner, but our guest, remaining with us only until we are satisfied that you are acting in good faith."

"You would hold me as a hostage!" cried Montezuma. "No, this is impossible. My subjects would not permit it. They would rise in war against you."

Alvarado and Leon, always short-tempered, became impatient.

"Let us tie the devil up and drag him through the streets like the heathen pig that he is," roared Alvarado.

"Or kill him here," said Leon.

Montezuma could not understand their words but he sensed their anger. Cortés held up his hand toward his men.

"You will have no trouble with your people, Lord Montezuma," he said, "if you come peacefully. You shall come in your litter, attended by your servants and courtiers. It will appear to be nothing more than a royal visit. And, of course, it is nothing more than that."

Finally the king sadly agreed. Borne by servants and accompanied by warriors and counselors, his golden litter was slowly carried through the streets to the Spaniards' quarters. He was given a large apartment and his servants waited on him as they did in his own palace. The only difference was that fully armed Spanish soldiers stood at all entrances, day and night.

At Montezuma's request the page, Orteguilla, was assigned to him as a companion. The boy had learned some of the Aztec language from Marina and could carry on simple conversations.

Montezuma was curious about the homeland

of the Spaniards. Orteguilla had grown up in the
Indies and had never seen Spain, but he tried to
answer the questions.

"Your king," asked Montezuma, "is he a priest
or warrior?"

"He is neither, my lord," answered Orteguilla.
"He is just a king. He has priests who perform
priestly duties and warriors who go to battle for
him."

"And when his warriors capture prisoners in

battle do his priests not sacrifice them in your temples?"

"Some times they are killed but they are not sacrificed."

When Orteguilla could no longer answer his questions, Montezuma would talk about himself.

"My name," he explained to the page, "means 'the sad one.' When I was your age I hoped to be nothing more than a priest. When the old counselors came to tell me that I was to succeed my uncle as king, I was sweeping the steps of the temple, and for a long time I could not believe that I was king. But as king I became a warrior and led my men into battle in distant places, in the hot countries far away and in the cold plateaus of our mountains.

"Always I have striven to make my nation strong and great, and I have sought to make our gods happy through sacrifice and prayer. Is this the way it is with your king?"

"Yes, my lord—at least I think so."

XXI

PUNISHMENT BY FIRE

A SENTRY stood rapping the butt of his lance on the stone floor outside Cortés' apartment. He waited and rapped again.

Finally Escobar came to the portal.

"You wanted the captain?" he asked.

"Yes," said the sentry. "Very important."

"What is it?"

"Quauhpopoca, the Indian chieftain who made the trouble at Villa Rica, is here. He has arrived with his principal men."

Escobar took the message to Cortés. Minutes later the Indian chieftain, followed by fifteen of his warriors, was ushered into Cortés' apartment. They were questioned closely. They denied that they had acted on Montezuma's orders but admitted that they were subject to him and did nothing of which he would disapprove.

Cortés sat in silence for a time; then, speaking

slowly and gravely, he announced that they would all be put to death by fire in the great plaza in front of the pyramid. He called in Pedro de Alvarado.

"Brother Alvarado," he said, "take some soldiers and go to the building at the foot of the pyramid. There you will find a great store of spears, arrows, darts and throwing slings. It is an arsenal that has been saved against time of war. Gather up all these weapons and stack them in a great pile here in the plaza outside our headquarters."

Alvarado saluted and left.

Orteguilla, the page, told Montezuma of these things as they happened. Montezuma listened and said nothing. Finally Cortés himself came to the king's apartment. He was followed by a soldier bearing chains.

"Lord Montezuma," he said, "these villainous vassals of yours have not only confessed the crime. They also have said they acted upon your orders. We are preparing to punish them by fire. We have told your people that this is done on your orders, and to avoid any chance of interference we are using for our fire the weapons, the arrows, and the

spears which you kept at the temple, weapons which you might turn against us."

"No, Malinche," said Montezuma. "They were only . . ."

"Do not interrupt me, Lord Montezuma. You, too, were guilty in this treachery. Only because we are compassionate are you spared from the flames. But you, too, must be punished."

Cortés nodded to the soldier who accompanied him. He stepped forward and quickly fastened iron shackles to the king's legs.

"You cannot do this," cried Montezuma. "You must not do it." But Cortés and the soldier were already gone. The king wept and his servants tried to comfort him.

Orteguilla walked to the embrasure and watched the scene in the plaza. The spears and arrows, broken, had been placed in a huge pile on the stone pavement of the plaza. The Indian chieftain and his fifteen confederates, tied hand and foot, were carried out and placed on top of the pile. A Spanish priest stood at one side, praying. Spanish soldiers ran forward with blazing pine torches and threw them into the pile of broken spears and arrows. The fire caught quickly, and the bodies of the Indians were hidden by flame and smoke.

Montezuma had become calm again and asked Orteguilla what was happening. Orteguilla described the scene.

"Do they cry out with pain or fear?" Montezuma asked.

"No, my lord, they are silent."

"And what of my people?"

"They, too, are silent. There are many thousands of them, but they only stand and watch."

Then Montezuma, too, was silent, staring into space.

Late in the day Cortés returned to Montezuma's apartment. He knelt on the floor in front of the king and with his own hands removed the shackles and threw them into a corner.

"The punishment is finished, Lord Montezuma. The treachery has been avenged. Now, if you like, you may return to your own palace."

Montezuma remained silent for a time. Then he spoke, slowly and deliberately.

"No, Malinche. I will never return to my palace. I will stay here with you. For if I return some of my warriors will insist that we make war upon you, a war which could bring only ruin to all of us. But if I am here and not among them they will not act. My greatest wish, Malinche, is that we, all of us, live in peace."

The king who had been, a week earlier, all-powerful, was now a sad and broken man.

XXII

THE DISPLEASED GODS

THERE FOLLOWED six months of peace in the great valley of Mexico. Montezuma seemed to accept willingly his position as a captive king. He held court as usual, received ambassadors from other Indian nations and issued orders exacting tribute from his vassal states — always under the watchful eyes of the Spaniards. He came to know each of the Spaniards by name and provided each one with servants to cook for him and make him comfortable. One of his favorites was Pedro de Alvarado, the hot-tempered one. Because of Alvarado's fiery hair and beard he called him "Tonatiuh," the sun god.

He sent Indian guides out with the Spaniards to show them the rivers where gold-bearing sands were found. When he learned that the Spaniards had found the treasure room in the palace of Axayacatl, he told them that it was all for them,

that they might do with it as they liked. The
Spaniards melted the ornaments into golden bars
which they divided into shares, putting aside a
fifth for the king of Spain. The gold amounted,
they reckoned, to many, many millions of pesos
in value.

When one of Montezuma's nephews, Cacama,
who ruled the neighboring kingdom of Texcoco,
threatened to rebel against the Spaniards, Montezuma ordered his spies to capture him and throw
him in chains, a prisoner of the Spaniards.

Cortés wanted some ships built so that the
Spaniards could, if necessary, leave the city without
depending upon the causeways which the Aztecs
could easily control. Montezuma ordered trees cut
from the royal forest and put a force of native artisans to work under the direction of a Spanish
shipbuilder. When the two little ships were com-
pleted, Montezuma and his courtiers went sailing
on the lake with the Spaniards, marveling at the
speed of the sailing vessels and the Spaniards' skill
in handling them.

At the suggestion of Cortés, Montezuma ordered an estate prepared for the Spanish king.
Houses were erected. The land was planted with
corn and cacao. Artificial lakes were built and
stocked with ducks and fish.

When Cortés asked for information about rivers
and harbors along the coasts, Montezuma sent out
observers and put artists to work drawing maps.

In everything, Montezuma seemed to try to
please the men who had made him a prisoner.

Winter in the valley of Mexico was cool and
dry. In the night cold winds came down from the

mountains, and the Spaniards huddled over small wood fires in their stone palace. During the day the sun was bright and hot, and the Spaniards walked about the city, marveling at the advanced culture of the Aztecs, far ahead of anything they had found among the rude Indians of the West Indies. The Aztecs were proficient in astronomy, had their own calendar system, maintained courts of law and schools for their children and showed great skill in their building. Many of the palaces and dwellings in the city were the equal of anything the Spaniards had known in Europe. A system of aqueducts brought a constant supply of fresh spring water into the city from the wooded heights of Chapultepec on the western shore of the lake where Montezuma had his summer palace amid great groves of cypress trees.

The more they saw of them the more the Spaniards admired the Aztecs. But they could not forgive their worship of idols, and nothing the Spaniards could do or say persuaded the Aztecs to cease making human sacrifices to their gods.

Finally Cortés asked Montezuma if the Spaniards could move their chapel from the underground room in the palace to the top of the pyramid in the great plaza. Reluctantly Montezuma agreed. The Spaniards went to the temple assigned to them on the pyramid, scrubbed it clean of blood, erected a chapel and decorated it with flowers. Daily they went here for prayers, marching solemnly in a body up the steps of the pyramid. They hoped that the sight would inspire the Aztecs to drop their old religion and take up the new.

But it seemed to have the opposite effect. Orteguilla, the page, was the first to notice the
change. Until now the king had wanted Orteguilla
near him at all times. Now, when the Aztec nobles
came to call upon their king, Montezuma would
order Orteguilla from the room.

Finally the Aztec emperor summoned Cortés
to his quarters.

"Malinche," said Montezuma after a long silence, "I have treated you as a brother. I have
rendered you the respect due one who is descended
from the gods. When you wanted gold, I gave you
gold. I have paid homage to your king and have
ordered my people to do the same. In everything
I have tried to please you, and my people, who
revere me as their king, have done as I have done.
But the gods of my people are more important
than I, and to say the truth, Malinche, our gods
are displeased by the desecration of our temples.
We do not say that your gods are bad gods. They
are good gods for you, and our gods are good for
us. But through the priests, our gods have told my
people that they must rise and seize you and sacrifice you in our temples to make amends for the
desecration that has occurred.

"I have restrained them, Malinche. But if I
should raise one finger they would spring to arms,
tens and hundreds of thousands of warriors, and
women and children and old people too, in a holy
war which could bring only disaster. They may do
it without my orders. The gods are very angry."

Cortés listened carefully, frowning.

"If it is as you say, Lord Montezuma, we shall
go, because we prefer not to stay if we cannot

have our shrine to worship our own God in our own fashion. But before we leave this land to go back across the waters we must build ships to replace those we destroyed. This will take time."

For the first time in many months Montezuma looked cheerful.

"I will send you an army of our best artisans, Malinche, to build these ships for you. When all is in readiness I will assign porters to carry your gold to the shore of the sea and warriors to guide you in safety. For it would grieve me, Malinche, if anything should happen to you and your brother soldiers."

XXIII

CEMPOALA

FROM THE fall of 1519 to the spring of 1520 Cortés had had an easy time of it in Tenochtitlán. Then, suddenly, everything began to go wrong.

First Montezuma told him he must leave the country in order to appease the angry Aztec gods. Cortés did not intend to do so, but before he had time to make up his mind how he should meet this crisis he was faced with another, more serious threat. In this case his enemies were not Indians, but Spaniards like himself.

Diego Velásquez, governor of Cuba, had fretted and stormed over Cortés' disobedience. He had learned of Cortés' action in setting up an independent colony in New Spain responsible directly to the crown rather than to himself. And he had learned of the rich shipload of treasure Cortés had sent back to Spain, treasure from which Velásquez got neither credit nor a share. He could imagine

Cortés finding more and more treasure and winning more favor with the royal court of Spain. He implored friends in Spain to discredit Cortés in the king's eyes, and meanwhile he planned another expedition, this one to capture Cortés and take charge of whatever additional treasure he had found.

Panfilo Narvaez, an arrogant soldier who was friendly with and loyal to the Cuban governor, was selected to head the expedition. He was given 18 ships and 900 men, including 80 horsemen, 80 musketeers and 150 crossbowmen, plus ample stores of cannon, ammunition and supplies.

On April 23, 1520, the expedition anchored off the island of San Juan de Ulua, the same anchorage Cortés had once used. One of the search parties found the garrison that Cortés had left at Villa Rica. It was now commanded by Gonzalo de Sandoval, the able young soldier whom Cortés was beginning to trust with difficult tasks.

Sandoval welcomed the search party, but when its members referred to Cortés and his followers as traitors and thieves, Sandoval was enraged. He and his men overcame the visitors in a brief scuffle. He then ordered Indian servants to tie them up in net hammocks. When all were securely trussed he had Indian porters load them on their backs and start the long overland march to Tenochtitlán, where they were to be delivered to Cortés.

Cortés met the Indian porters and their curious loads on the outskirts of Tenochtitlán. He ordered that the prisoners be untied and apologized for the rude treatment they had been given. Taking them with him to his quarters, he fed them and gave them gifts of gold chains and ingots. He showed them the wonders of Tenochtitlán—the great pyramids and the fine houses—and introduced them to the captive king, Montezuma, explaining that by holding Montezuma he could control the entire country.

"You see, my friends," he said, "all these wonders and riches lie within our hands. Here in this city alone there is more than enough for us and you too. If Spaniards fight Spaniards these Indians will know it; they will rise and take advantage of our enmity, and all will be lost, including, perhaps, our lives. Far better for all if we unite and reap this golden harvest together."

Narvaez' men were convinced. They set off on their long trip back to San Juan de Ulua, determined to persuade their leader to join forces with Cortés.

But Cortés knew Narvaez and many of the men around him, and he was certain that the leader of the new expedition would never accept anything short of complete surrender by Cortés and his men.

So he too prepared to march to the coast. He left a garrison in Tenochtitlán and placed Pedro de Alvarado in charge, cautioning him to control his temper and exercise good judgment. He took with him only seventy men, and Montezuma, carried in his golden litter, came to the beginning of the causeway to bid him good-by.

On the way to the coast Cortés was joined by 120 men commanded by Juan Velásquez de Leon, who had been off on a scouting expedition. He went through the city of Tlascala, where he was granted a reinforcement of 600 fresh Indian troops.

Before the army had proceeded many miles, however, the Tlascalan warriors slipped away, one after another, and returned to their homes. They were willing to fight their bitter enemies, the Aztecs, but they had no desire to fight more Spaniards.

Cortés could count only on the small garrison at Villa Rica commanded by Gonzalo de Sandoval. At the most he could raise no more than one quarter of the force that was commanded by Narvaez.

Narvaez, meanwhile, had taken quarters in the town of Cempoala, still ruled by the fat chieftain whom Cortés had found so helpful. Confident that Cortés, with his greatly reduced army, could cause him no trouble, Narvaez lived a life of ease and paid no attention to the complaints of the fat chieftain that his soldiers, unlike those of Malinche, were stealing from the Indians.

Cortés, nearing Cempoala, sent envoys to Narvaez to see if a peaceful settlement could be made. Narvaez scorned the offer, and Cortés prepared to attack.

It was now the rainy season. Rain fell each day and often continued through the night. Cortés picked a rainy night for the attack, reasoning that Narvaez, who liked comfort, would least expect it then. His ragged followers armed themselves with long, copper-tipped lances which Cortés had ordered one of the Indian tribes to make for him; only thus, he knew, would his foot soldiers stand a chance against Narvaez' horsemen.

They forded a stream near the town. Swollen with rains, it was dangerous and two of Cortés' men were lost. But again he reasoned that Narvaez

would least expect him to attack in such a fashion.

The ragged men crept through the mud and the dripping forest. They surprised two of Narvaez' guards outside the town. One they captured but the other ran shouting into Cempoala. So confident was Narvaez that Cortés would not dare attack him that he paid no attention to the guard. Only when Cortés and his men were silently stalking through the streets of the city was a general alarm given.

With a shout Cortés and his men attacked. Sandoval, with a picked group of men, charged the pyramid that was occupied by Narvaez. Musketeers at the summit fired at them, but the musket balls whistled over the heads of Sandoval's men. Without giving the musketeers time to reload they sprang up the steps of the pyramid, knocked over the defenders and threw a pine torch into the thatched roof shelter in which Narvaez was hiding. In a few minutes they captured Narvaez, and the fighting in the streets below was soon over. A swarm of beetles that gave off a phosphoric light like fireflies had swept into the town. Narvaez' men, thinking them to be the match fires of muskets, believed that Cortés must have at least a thousand musketeers. They gave up.

Narvaez, who had been wounded in one eye, was brought before Cortés.

"This victory must give you great satisfaction," he said.

Cortés looked at him coldly and replied: "There is much for which I am thankful, but this victory over you is the least of our accomplishments in this wild country."

He then went out into the night to visit various detachments of Narvaez' army to see if they would join forces with him. All were willing, and as he walked back to his own quarters Cortés added up the Spanish force he now had at his command: more than a thousand soldiers, well equipped with horses, cannon, muskets, powder. With such a force and the Indian allies he could command, he could conquer the whole of New Spain. He could strengthen the garrison at Tenochtitlán, guarding Montezuma; he could march to the ocean that he knew lay in the west.

XXIV

REBELLION

WHILE CORTES was busy strengthening his position at Villa Rica, he received alarming news from Tenochtitlán. Montezuma's subjects were in a state of rebellion. Alvarado sent word that the Aztecs had surrounded the palace, shut off supplies of food and water and burned the two ships built for the Spaniards.

Cortés organized his new force with all possible speed. The men who had been wounded in the battle at Cempoala were left behind in the garrison at Villa Rica, while Cortés led the rest in a forced march on Tenochtitlán. With plenty of supplies and with no interference from the natives, they arrived within a week at the causeway on which they had made their first entrance to the city.

This time all was quiet. Cortés halted his troops and had a trumpeter sound a signal. The clear notes of the trumpet floated out over the lake and toward the city. In a few minutes the sound of a cannon saluted them. Their companions were still alive.

The army moved forward along the causeway. The city seemed completely deserted. There were no canoes on the canals and no people in the streets. As the Spaniards advanced along the broad, empty avenue, their footsteps echoed in the silence. They swung into the palace of Axayacatl, their old headquarters, where their comrades greeted them, many with tears in their eyes. Cortés went immediately to his apartment and sent for Pedro de Alvarado.

"Now, tell me what has happened," said Cortés.

"You had not been long gone, my captain, when some of the Indian nobles came to see me. They said it was time for one of their principal feasts of the year, the incensing of the Hummingbird Wizard. It is an occasion for ceremonial dancing, competitions and festivities which they have always held on the great pyramid and in the plaza, just opposite our quarters. They asked our permission to hold the feast.

"I talked with Montezuma and he said this festival was very important to his people and that they should be allowed to go ahead with it. I gave the permission, but I did not trust them. I thought that this might be an occasion for them to try to liberate Montezuma and overthrow our garrison.

"When the day of the festival arrived, I had our men stationed through the plaza, well-armed and open-eyed. The festival began shortly after dawn with much eating and drinking. Then the dancing began, and a wilder scene you have never witnessed, my captain. The drums beat faster and faster, the flutes played louder and louder, and the warriors danced and screamed—just as in battle. They would leap in the air and shake their fists. And then they would point toward our headquarters here and scream some more.

"It seemed to me," Alvarado continued, "that they were working themselves up to a pitch, and would assault the palace and try to take Montezuma. So I gave my men a signal and we fell upon them with our swords. Our men at the gates to the plaza leveled their muskets on them and fired, and our pikemen did excellent work in skewering those who attempted to flee. There were at least six hundred of them, my captain, and only a handful of us."

"Were they armed?" Cortés asked.

"No . . ."

"Oh, Alvarado, you great fool! Did you suppose they would attack with their bare fists?"

Alvarado hung his head and was silent.

"And the dancers wore their finest gowns, their finest jewels?"

"Yes." Alvarado continued to look down at the floor.

"And I suppose that having massacred them you and your men then robbed the bodies?"

Alvarado nodded his head and Cortés struck his forehead with the palm of his hand.

"Well, what happened next?"

"We retreated in good form to the palace and went about our duties. For a time everything was silent. Then we could hear people wailing as they came and dragged the bodies away.

"I put our men on the alert and we stood double guard all night long. In the early morning hours that great drum on the pyramid began sounding and in the distance we could hear people shouting. There was a great blaze on the shore of the lake and by looking from the walls we could see that they had destroyed our boats.

"And at first light they attacked us, my captain, streaming up the street and across the plaza, hurling spears and stones and shooting arrows into the courtyard. We stood them off with little difficulty, but many of us suffered wounds, and seven of our men were killed . . . and many Tlascalans. Finally I begged Montezuma to speak to them. He went to the wall and urged them to cease their fighting. He explained that in battling us they were endangering his life. They stopped fighting then, but they have brought us no food and they have closed their market places and cut the pipe that brought us water from the aqueduct.

"They are fierce warriors, my captain, more fierce by far than the Tabascans or the Tlascalans. But they have not attacked again. They probably thought they had us securely caught, like a fly in a wine bottle; and that we would either die here or be forced out by hunger. But now that you have come with reinforcements, they may attack again."

XXV

A WEEK OF BATTLE

DURING THE night Cortés made plans and issued orders.

He issued an order to the Aztecs to reopen
their markets immediately, sending the message by
a kinsman of Montezuma who had been staying
with him. The Aztec noble took the message, de-
parted and never returned.

He wrote a message to his garrison at Villa
Rica, telling them of his safe return and of the
situation in Tenochtitlán, a situation which he soon
hoped to correct. He handed the message to a
Tlascalan runner and bade him Godspeed. The
runner left in the gray light of dawn, but within
less than a half-hour he was back, breathless.

"Master," he said, "they have removed all
bridges from the causeways and are preparing to
attack."

Climbing to the roof of the palace, Cortés

could hear the hum of voices, like a swarm of
bees, and in every direction he could see Indians
approaching the palace. The streets were black with
people; the surfaces of the canals were covered with
loaded canoes. The drum on the pyramid was
sounding again and the sound of flutes rose from
the advancing mob. Cortés ran back down to the
courtyard and ordered his men to their posts.

The Spanish musketeers and artillerymen
waited on the walls, watching the advancing sea of
screaming faces. The Indian nobles, with their wild
animal helmets, and the common soldiers, wearing
white cotton head bands, rolled forward. Arms
brandished bows and spears while others waved
pikes with battle flags and plumes of feathers. The
Spaniards held their fire until the horde was within a few yards of the palace wall. Then they fired
in unison and the first files of the Aztec fell to the
street. The Indians had heard the Spaniards fire
their guns, but few of them had ever seen the
damage they could do. However, they hesitated
only a moment, then swept forward again.

Meanwhile the flat roofs of nearby buildings,
which had been bare only a few minutes before,
swarmed with Aztec warriors. Some were armed
with leather slings with which they hurled stones
into the courtyard of the palace. Others had throwing sticks with which they could propel a spear
with tremendous force. Though the Spaniards were
protected by their armor, the force of the stones
knocked many of them to the ground, and the
spears and arrows began to find crevices in their
armor. The Tlascalans, protected only by cotton
armor, suffered heavily.

The fighting went on and on until sunset. Suddenly the great drum stopped and the attacks ceased. The Aztecs dragged their dead away and the Spaniards sat down wearily to munch on a few grains of corn. Some of them started digging a well in the courtyard.

At daybreak the Aztecs attacked again, just as they had on the day before, and Cortés ordered his men to prepare for the offensive. First the guns were fired into the ranks of the Indians, clearing a bloody path. A trumpet sounded inside the palace, the gates swung open. The Spanish horsemen, led by Cortés himself, and followed by Tlascalan warriors, charged out into the plaza. The Aztecs retreated slowly; many of them were trampled under the horses' hoofs. The horsemen pushed them back until they reached a wooden barricade that had been erected across one of the streets. The Spaniards tried to break the barricade so that the pursuit could be continued, but meanwhile fresh Aztec troops were attacking from a side street. The Indians unhorsed one Spaniard and sought to drag him into a canoe, but Cortés rode into the midst of them, scattered the warriors and helped the horseman to remount.

Finally the Spaniards retreated to the palace. At sundown the fighting ceased as before, but the Aztecs, instead of withdrawing, camped close to the palace wall and began a wild, wailing chant.

"Come, Orteguilla," Cortés said to his page, "you understand a little of this heathen language. What is it they are saying?"

"They are saying," replied Orteguilla, white-faced, "that their gods have delivered us to them, that the sacrificial stone is ready and that their knives are sharp. And that our hearts will be placed on the altar of the Hummingbird Wizard and that our bodies will be thrown to their caged animals, and that . . ."

"That is enough, Orteguilla."

At dawn, the following day, the Aztecs placed huge timbers against the palace wall and began climbing over, dropping into the courtyard with their obsidian swords and copper-tipped lances. There was no room for gunfire, so the Spaniards fell upon them with their swords and knocked down the scaling timbers.

The Spaniards moved slowly and with effort. All were weak from hunger and sleeplessness, and their gunpowder was running low. Cortés knew that they could not hold out for long. He went to see Montezuma, and asked him if he would intercede to stop the fighting.

"No, Malinche. They hate you and they no longer trust me, their king, because I have been friendly with you. Neither you nor I will leave this palace alive. Nor have I any desire to."

"But Lord Montezuma, if your people will give us only one day of peace and a little food we will depart quietly and all this death and destruction will end."

Finally Montezuma agreed and mounted the wall, wearing his golden diadem. He held out his arms. The screams died away and the drum was silent.

"Listen, my people. Let us put an end to the fighting, the useless shedding of blood. Malinche has agreed to leave our city with all his men, his strange weapons and animals. He will go back to the land of his fathers and Mexico will again be as it was. Return to your homes, lay down your arms and see that a way is clear for Malinche to depart." The crowd was attentive. If Montezuma had said no more, the battle might have ended. But he went on:

"If you thought me a prisoner of Malinche, then you did right in making war. But you are mistaken. I am not his prisoner. He is my guest and my friend. I have been free to leave at any time but I have stayed with my friend."

There was a murmur from the crowd. Suddenly a voice in the plaza shouted: "They have made a coward of you, an old woman." Other voices took up the cry and a cloud of arrows and stones flew toward the palace wall. Montezuma was struck by three stones and fell, unconscious. The drum boomed again and the angry voices screamed as the attack was resumed.

Cortés went to his quarters and talked to the Spanish priest who was tending Montezuma.

"How is he?"

"He will not let us treat his wounds and he tears away the bandages," the priest answered. "His wounds are severe, but he is afflicted more by the rejection of his people. He has a broken heart and does not wish to live."

Meanwhile a body of Aztec warriors was gathering on the great pyramid opposite the Spanish quarters. From their elevated position they discharged clouds of arrows on the Spanish garrison, so that no one could expose himself for an instant without danger. Cortés quickly realized that the enemy must be driven off the pyramid if the Spaniards wished to remain in control of their quarters.

Calling to Escobar, he assigned him a hundred men to storm the pyramid and set fire to the shrines. Escobar and his followers dashed from the gate of the palace and raced across the plaza toward the pyramid. Cortés watched from an opening in his apartment. Suddenly from the back side of the pyramid a group of at least 500 Aztec warriors appeared. They ran forward to meet Escobar and his men. The Spaniards fought bravely with their swords, but they were slowly forced back toward the palace.

Cortés tied a round shield to his wounded left arm and led a group of horsemen out of the palace gate to charge the Aztecs. They drove them back, inflicting heavy losses, but the horses could not maintain their footing on the slippery stone pavement. The Spaniards had to send them back to the palace and charge ahead on foot.

The Aztecs retreated toward the pyramid, ran to the first tier, fought furiously there, retreated to the next tier and the next until finally they had reached the top. The Spaniards battled them all the way. On the flat summit of the pyramid the battle went on. Much of it was hand-to-hand combat. Spaniards and Aztec would grapple together, drop their weapons and roll together over the edge. Finally the only Aztecs left were three priests, their black hair crusted with the blood of the morning's sacrifices. The Spaniards seized the priests, knocked over the hideous idols and rolled them down the sides of the pyramid. Finally they put torches to the wooden temple itself. As the flames and smoke rose high in the air there was a wail of grief from the Aztecs in the plaza below.

That night Cortés and his men rode out into the city and set fire to three hundred houses. It was their day of greatest success, but they had lost forty-five of their men in the fighting on the pyramid.

The next day Cortés invited the principal chiefs and their followers to a parley. Accompanied by Marina, he mounted the wall, motioned for silence and spoke to the thousands of warriors below.

"We have killed and crippled you, burned your houses and destroyed your gods. You have brought this on yourselves. But because your ruler,

Montezuma, is my friend, I will stay my hand if you will lay down your weapons and return to your homes. Otherwise I will make your city a smoking ruins, a city of the dead."

One of the Aztec chieftains below shouted a reply.

"Oh, treacherous Malinche, you have killed many of us. Yet look about you: as far as your eye can see our city is still full of warriors. We lose many, yes, but like a spring of water we always have more. You, when you lose one man, are weaker. If we buy one of your lives with a thousand of our own, we will gladly do so. There is no escape, Malinche. You are doomed."

There was a roar from the crowd in the plaza and the battle went on again.

Cortés decided that if the Spaniards must leave Tenochtitlán their safest exit would be over the shortest of the three causeways, the one leading to the west. But between their palace and the beginning of the causeway there were seven canals, and the bridge over each of them had been destroyed.

The Spaniards, led by the cavalry, fought their way to the first of the destroyed canal bridges. Stones and timbers from ruined houses were thrown into the canal until the gap was filled. They went on across, filled in the next and the next, until they reached the beginning of the causeway. The work of repairing the bridges occupied two whole days, and the Spaniards were under constant attack by the Aztecs.

When they finally returned to headquarters, they learned of the death of Montezuma. Spurning all attempts to comfort him, the Indian monarch had also rejected the Spaniards' efforts to convert him to Christianity. The Spaniards placed his body in the royal litter. The Aztec courtiers who had remained with their king then sorrowfully carried the litter out of the Spaniards' quarters and back to Montezuma's own palace, which he had left so many months before. For a time the plaza and the streets were empty and silent. Then the fighting began again in even greater bitterness.

Cortés called his men together in the courtyard.

"The Lord Montezuma is dead," he said, "and we have lost our best hope of peaceful conquest. Conquer we will, but we cannot fight here with neither supplies nor freedom of movement. Tonight after midnight we will leave this place, proceeding by the western causeway, which is shorter than the others. We have built a portable bridge with which we will cross the gaps in the causeway where the bridges have been destroyed. After all have passed one gap, the portable bridge will be carried forward to the next. We must stay together in close order.

"There is gold for all in the treasure room. The royal fifth has been set aside for Don Carlos, our king, and a special guard will be in charge of transporting it. Great quantities remain. Let each man take a share—whatever he likes. But remember that he who carries little travels faster and farther. And remember that we shall come back to Tenochtitlán. There will be all this and more."

The weary men cheered and crowded into the treasure room, pawing over the gold and jewels. The men who had come with Narvaez were greedy and loaded themselves down. Cortés' veterans were more familiar with the sight of gold and with the hardships of travel. They took small things that could be easily carried.

Escobar stood holding a piece of golden chain. Near him one of Narvaez' men was busily stuffing heavy bars of gold into his waistband. "Is that all you are going to take?" he asked Escobar.

"No, I am taking something else, something more precious."

"What is that?" asked the man eagerly, wondering if he had missed something.

"My life," said Escobar, and walked away, whirling the chain.

XXVI

THE SAD NIGHT

THE EARLY morning hours of July 1, 1520, were to go down in Spanish history as *la noche triste,* the sad night.

All retreats are sad and many are disastrous. This was both.

The night was dark and wet. Gusts of wind swept down from the mountains and sent sheets of rain through the streets of Tenochtitlán, hissing on the smoking ruins and washing blood from the dark streets.

At midnight the Spaniards and their Tlascalan allies assembled in the courtyard. The Spanish priest said a mass and the Spanish soldiers prayed while the Tlascalans watched curiously. No one spoke above a whisper. Cortés had already given his marching orders. The lead was to be taken by Gonzalo de Sandoval, with 200 foot soldiers. A larger group of foot soldiers was to make up the rear guard, commanded by Pedro de Alvarado and Velásquez de Leon. Cortés was to command the center of the column, including the rest of the foot soldiers, the cannon, the baggage (large supplies of gold but no food) and the Aztec hostages, three of whom were children of Montezuma. The cavalry and the Tlascalan warriors were to be distributed all along the marching column. The arrangement was very orderly, but it was not to remain that way.

The gates were slowly eased open. No one spoke, and the horsemen walked their mounts. The plaza was dark, deserted and lonely in the rain. There was the occasional clink of armor and the muffled sound of the horses' hoofs. The bare feet of the Tlascalan warriors and porters could be heard slapping softly against the wet stones of the pavement.

All went well until they approached the beginning of the causeway, separated from the island city by a gap of open water. Once their portable bridge was laid across that gap they would be on their way to freedom and safety.

Suddenly a shrill whistle pierced the night. A second whistle sounded from another direction. Then there came the sound of conch shell trumpets and somewhere, off in the darkness, a drum began to throb.

Cortés spurred his horse to the front of the column where the Spaniards and Tlascalans were struggling to put the bridge in place.

"Hurry," he shouted, "the devils will soon be upon us."

Wheeling about on his horse, he dashed to the

rear of the column to make certain everyone was prepared for an attack, then returned to his own position in the center. The column began moving forward over the portable bridge.

Now there was a growing roar that seemed to come from all sides in the darkness. Looking back toward the plaza the Spaniards could see a great mass moving toward them; and in the lake on either side of the causeway they could dimly see the outlines of canoes. Arrows, darts and stones came whistling through the air toward the slowly moving army. Now the Aztecs were so close that their white tunics could be seen. Many crashed their canoes against the side of the causeway and sprang up to grapple with the refugees. Others had barbed darts attached to strong cords; when the dart embedded itself in Spaniard or Tlascalan, the Aztec would tug on the cord and topple his enemy into the water.

The forward guard reached the second gap in the causeway and halted to wait for the bridge to be brought up, fighting to maintain their foothold. As the column inched slowly forward, the causeway became packed with people, baggage and horses and some of the forward guard were pushed into the water. Many of the soldiers who had loaded themselves with gold sank out of sight; those who managed to stay afloat were seized by the Aztecs, loaded into canoes and taken away for sacrifice.

Finally the rear guard crossed the first gap and the soldiers struggled to lift the portable bridge. It would not move; the weight of the marching column had pushed it deep in the mud.

Meanwhile, at the head of the column the second gap began to be filled with wrecked canoes, bodies of men and horses, cannon, bales of cloth, hampers loaded with gold until finally it was shallow enough to be waded.

The column moved slowly forward, fighting in front and back and on both sides. Cortés tried to hurry his people along over the gap. He started to give a hand to Salazar, the page, when the boy was struck by a spear and dropped to the ground. The captain jumped from his horse to help him but Salazar was dead.

Cortés rode ahead to the third gap. Here there were not so many attackers. Some horsemen were swimming across, letting foot soldiers clutch their saddles. Some foot soldiers, discarding weapons and armor, tried to swim it alone but sank under the weight of the gold they carried.

Cortés again turned his horse and galloped to the rear. The rear guard was still trying to cross the second gap. Some had crossed but were surrounded by yelling Aztecs. Cortés rode into their midst, chopping with his sword. He saw Leon, who had once been his enemy but had become one of his most trusted lieutenants, go down under a mass of Indians.

Finally only Alvarado was left on the far side. The big red-headed man's horse had been killed by a spear thrust, and Alvarado was fighting on foot, his lance in one hand, his sword in the other. Indians were all around him and Aztec canoes had clustered in the water gap, shallow though it was. Finally Alvarado cleared a path for himself. Running forward, he gave a great shout, placed his

lance point in the middle of the gap and vaulted high over the heads of his enemy. The Spaniards around him gave a feeble cheer and went on with their fighting.

The sky was getting light in the east and the grim outlines of the buildings of Tenochtitlán could be seen, black against the gray sky. Cortés reached the mainland, dismounted and walked to a small temple. He seated himself on the steps in the shelter of a huge, gnarled cypress tree and watched the remnants of his army creep past.

Some of his most trusted men had been lost, but he watched the straggling column closely, hoping that by some miracle they might reappear. Most of the survivors were wounded, and all were wet and covered with mud. Most of them still clasped their swords, but many had lost their armor. Muskets, crossbows and cannon were gone. So were many of the horses. The baggage was gone, the hampers of gold, and even the Aztec hostages, Montezuma's children. Cortés tried to guess the extent of his loss. It appeared that at least 400, possibly 500, Spaniards had been either killed or dragged off to be sacrificed. And at least 4,000 of his Tlascalan allies had been either killed or captured.

Cortés dropped his head in his arms and wept.

XXVII

OTUMBA

THE SPANIARDS' only hope of safety, they knew, lay in the friendly region of Tlascala. But they were separated from Tlascala by the city of Tenochtitlán, from which they had just fled, and the great lake that surrounded it.

Slowly and painfully they began to work their way around the lake, first to the north, then to the east. Those unable to walk were carried on the backs of Tlascalan warriors.

Frequently they were attacked by roving bands of Aztecs, but the horsemen always drove them off. Far more serious was the lack of food. They found cornfields that had been stripped of grain, and they munched on dry cornstalks. When one of their horses was killed in a skirmish with the Aztecs, they cut up the meat, gnawed the bones and even chewed on the hide, trying to get nourishment.

On the seventh day they could still see Tenochtitlán far to the south of them. To the north were two great pyramids, apparently deserted. Ahead was a range of mountains beyond which lay Tlascala and, they hoped, safety, rest, comfort and food. But would the Tlascalans still be friendly? They had been friendly before because the Spaniards were a victorious army. Now they were returning, beaten.

As the soldiers struggled up the mountain slopes, the scouts who had gone ahead came running back with reports that just beyond the next range of hills, near a town called Otumba, a great army was waiting for them. The Spaniards groaned. Surely they would never reach Tlascala.

Cortés called a halt for the night and spoke to his men:

"This, gentlemen, is our greatest test. We are reduced in numbers, aching with wounds and misery. The Indians no longer fear us. They know that we are mortal and bleed and die as they do. They no longer fear our horses. They still, perhaps, fear our guns, but we no longer have guns. All the advantages we have enjoyed in the past are gone. All that we have left are our good swords, our Spanish spirit and the help of the Almighty, for which we must all devoutly pray." His voice, always strong and confident in the past, quavered as he spoke.

The Spaniards sat or lay on the ground during the night. Few of them slept.

At dawn they were up and marching toward a pass that cut through the range of hills and into the valley of Otumba. When the pass opened into the valley, they stopped and stared in bewilderment. Below them lay a great army, stretching away to the horizon. The enemy, despite the losses in the battles of Tenochtitlán, seemed to have put an entirely fresh force in the field. The tunics of the soldiers were sparkling white. The helmets of their leaders were new and unmarked; the red and green plumes on their helmets were brilliant and new. The sun glinted brightly on the obsidian edges of their swords and the copper tips of their lances.

Cortés arranged his men in a long, thin line facing the enemy. The horsemen were at each end.

"Strike for the chieftains," he said. "That is our only hope. We cannot possibly kill all the warriors, but without leaders they may lose their heart for fighting."

The Spanish line moved slowly forward. The Indians screamed and dashed toward Cortés and his men. With a strength few of them thought they had, the Spaniards plunged into the battle, thrusting with their swords. The horsemen left the Spanish line and charged into the close-packed Indians, trampling them underfoot and making paths for the foot soldiers. The Spaniards held their own, but fresh Indian troops kept pouring into the line, and the little group of Spaniards and Tlascalans was tossed back and forth like a chip of wood in the waves.

The sun climbed, stood overhead and began to decline, and as it did the Indians slowly began pushing the Spaniards back toward the pass through which they had entered the valley. The Spaniards knew that if they were forced into the pass they would be hemmed in and slaughtered.

Cortés' horse was speared and fell to the ground. The Spanish captain then mounted a big, heavy horse that had been used for baggage. From his new mount he saw, not far away, a chieftain who was more finely dressed than the rest. He was surrounded by a group of nobles, one of whom held aloft a golden staff with a flag of golden netting. Cortés recognized it as the standard of an army commander. He spurred his heavy pack horse and, followed by four other horsemen, dashed forward toward the close-packed Indians. Thrusting with his lance, he broke through the ring of nobles that encircled the leader and ran him through with his lance.

A great wail arose from the Indian army. Overcome by sudden terror, they thought only of escape, trampling on one another in their haste to get away.

The Spaniards followed after, taking their revenge, until the enemy had completely abandoned the battlefield. The whole valley, littered with bodies and broken weapons, was thrown into shadow as the sun dropped behind the range of hills. Here and there golden ornaments shone brightly on the bodies of fallen Indians.

"Come," Cortés gave the order, "let us leave this place. We have met an army of 200,000 men and we have conquered them. Conquerors do not lie in the filth of the battle. And conquerors we are; nothing in this savage land can withstand us."

The weary little band trudged on toward Tlascala.

XXVIII

THE LAST STEP

THE FORTUNES of the Spaniards had reached their lowest point just before the battle of Otumba. Now, although there were still many battles to be fought and many weary miles to be marched, victory was certain.

They crossed into the Republic of Tlascala, where they were welcomed in friendly fashion; the Tlascalans were still their allies, despite the defeat. They rested, treated their wounds and ate. Their spirits improved and some wanted to return to Cuba and forget about Mexico. Cortés talked with them and promised that things would' be better.

And their situation did begin to improve. Other ships arrived on the east coast. Some carried adventurers who had heard of the great riches of New Spain. Others were sent out by the Cuban governor, Diego Velásquez, who still wanted to arrest Cortés. But all joined forces with Cortés in the

Tlascalan capital, bringing horses, guns, gunpowder and other needed supplies. After a time Cortés' army was larger than ever. He sent out expeditions to conquer nearby towns that remained loyal to the Aztecs. And he laid plans for the reconquest of Tenochtitlán.

To do this he needed a navy as well as an army. He sent to Villa Rica for the rigging that had been saved from the scuttled ships. He sent thousands of Tlascalans into the mountains to cut logs of cedar and cypress, while others worked in the pine forests making pitch to calk the seams of the vessels. Some of the Spaniards were familiar with shipbuilding and they taught Tlascalan workmen how to shape the logs into planks for the ships. Thirteen little brigantines took shape in the city of Tlascala. When they were finished, the men took them apart again. Each part was clearly marked so that the ships could be quickly reassembled.

The Spaniards then marched on the city of Texcoco. Situated on the eastern shore of the lake that surrounded Tenochtitlán, it was allied to the Aztec empire. The Texcocan ruler and many of his subjects fled toward Tenochtitlán. The Spaniards occupied the city without difficulty and installed another king.

A small army of Tlascalans then took the shaped timbers of the dismantled ships and marched over the mountains to Texcoco, where the ships were reassembled and launched. One of them proved to be top-heavy, but the rest were seaworthy. Thus Cortés had a fleet of twelve vessels.

Cortés, meanwhile, reconnoitered the valley.

First he skirted the lake around the northern edge, going as far as Tacuba, the place where the retreat across the causeway had ended. Returning to Texcoco, he next set out around the southern edge of the lake. He crossed the mountains and went as far south as a town called Cuernavaca. He then turned north, came again to Tacuba and returned to Texcoco, having completely circled Tenochtitlán.

Almost everywhere he went there were battles. But the Spaniards were refreshed and stronger than ever before and they had little trouble. Cortés recruited new allies from towns that hated and feared the Aztecs and wanted the protection of the Spaniards, and he learned more of the country than he had known on his first trip to Tenochtitlán.

He also learned what had happened in the Aztec capital.

After the death of Montezuma, his brother, Cuitlahua, had been named king. He had directed the assault on the Spaniards as they retreated across the causeway, and had also ordered the battle of Otumba. But after a few months he had died in an epidemic of smallpox. The Spaniards had brought the disease to the New World and the Indians had neither resistance to it nor knowledge of how to treat it.

Cuitlahua was succeeded by Cuauhtemoc, his nephew, who had married one of Montezuma's daughters. Cuauhtemoc was young, intelligent and a brave warrior. He was fierce and proud and had vowed never to surrender to the Spaniards. To this day Cuauhtemoc is one of the national heroes of Mexico.

Cortés decided that Tenochtitlán could only be

taken by siege. The city was dependent upon the surrounding countryside for food and supplies which had to be brought in across the causeways or carried in by canoes.

His fleet could control the water-borne traffic. His army he split into three divisions. One, commanded by Pedro de Alvarado, he stationed at the end of the Tacuba causeway. Another, under Gon-

zalo de Sandoval, he placed at the end of the
northern causeway; and he himself took a position
on the third causeway, the one by which they had
originally entered the city. Each of the leaders commanded a force of about 30 horsemen, 170 foot
soldiers and some thousands of Indian allies.

Before sending his lieutenants off to their posts,
Cortés gave them final instructions. They were not
going to try to take the city by storm. They
would, instead, starve it into submission. They were
to make sorties along the causeways, possibly going
into the city itself, but always returning to their
bases rather than making a stand in the city. The
Indian allies were to be restrained; if possible Cortés wanted to take the city without further damage.

He embraced Alvarado and Sandoval and sent
them off to their posts. "This," he said, "is the last
step of our long journey."

XXIX

END OF TENOCHTITLÁN

THE SPANIARDS had thought the last step would be a quick one. But the Aztecs, as tough-minded as the Spanish themselves, continued to fight long after all hope was gone.

At first the little fleet of brigantines had an easy time of it, ramming the canoes that were taking supplies into the besieged city. Then the Aztecs secretly drove wooden stakes in the bottom of the lake. The brigantines, pursuing the canoes, went aground on the stakes. While the Spaniards labored to free their ships, the Aztecs attacked them mercilessly.

At each of the gaps along the causeways, the Aztecs had destroyed the bridges and built fortifications on the city side of the breaks. When the Spaniards attacked along the causeways, they would bring their brigantines alongside and use their cannon to clear the Aztecs away from behind the fortifications. The crews from the brigantines would then mount the causeway, wreck the fortifications and throw the stones and timbers down in the gap so that the horsemen and foot soldiers could pass.

But during the night, when the Spaniards had retreated to their quarters, the Aztecs would return, clear the wreckage out of the gap and rebuild their fortifications, so that on the next day the Spaniards had all their work to do over again.

Time and again the Spaniards, attacking from all three causeways at once, fought their way into

the city. But they were under continuous attacks. The Aztecs fought in the streets, along the canals and from the rooftops.

Gradually the proud city was becoming a ruin. Buildings were burned so that the Aztecs could not fight from their rooftops. Others were wrecked to provide materials to fill in the canals. Public buildings were destroyed to break the spirit of the people and temples were wrecked to show the Aztecs that their gods would not protect them.

The Spaniards built a catapult to hurl huge stones against the buildings from which the Aztecs were fighting. But when the catapult threw the first great stone high in the air, the boulder fell back on the catapult itself, wrecking it. The Aztecs, who

had watched from a distance, laughed and screamed insults at the Spaniards.

Fighting back and forth along the causeways, many of the Spaniards were seized and carried away in canoes. Later, their comrades watching from a distance, could see them being led up the steps of the pyramids to be sacrificed.

But gradually the Aztecs weakened. They were completely without food from the outside world; their supply of drinking water had been cut off; they chewed twigs and bark to ease their hunger and hunted eagerly for rats and lizards to eat. The collection of rare birds and wild animals that Montezuma had kept for amusement had long since been killed for food. Disease and hunger had so weakened the living that they were not strong enough to bury the dead. And all the while the city was crumbling around the desperate Indians.

Now the Spaniards could come freely into the center of the city, wrecking buildings and temples as they came, filling in the canals to give them room to maneuver with their horses. The Aztecs still scowled at them fiercely from the few remaining buildings and hurled darts and stones. But they had no strength and their aim was poor. Their faces were haggard and filthy and their once-fine garments hung on them in dirty tatters.

Three times Cuauhtemoc rejected, scornfully, Cortés' invitation to surrender and save himself and what was left of his city and his people. Finally, on August 13, 1521, the Spaniards made a last assault on the Aztecs who remained in the city. Cortés delayed the attack, giving the survivors one last chance to surrender. They spurned it. Although many of them were too weak to stand, they still tried to hurl their spears and darts at the white men. Some, trying to charge toward the hated foreigners, fell to the ground or tumbled into the canal. At last Cortés gave a signal to his Indian allies and they fell upon the survivors without mercy. Many of the Spaniards faced the other way, unable to watch the slaughter.

Spaniards on one of the brigantines, cruising on the lake, saw a large canoe leaving the ruined, smoking city. The commander turned his ship toward it and ordered his crossbowmen to be prepared to shoot.

A young Aztec stood up in the stern of the canoe. His cheeks were hollow and his long cotton gown hung on him in ragged ribbons. But he spoke with dignity.

"I am Cuauhtemoc," he said. "Take me to Malinche. I am his prisoner."

XXX

MEXICO BECOMES A
FREE NATION

THE OLD city of Tenochtitlán was leveled to the ground and a new city was built upon the ruins. Though Spanish, it still had in it much of the ancient Aztec city. Where the pyramids had been, churches were built with the stones from the pyramids and the shattered idols. Where the Aztec rulers' palaces had stood, new palaces for the Spanish colonial rulers rose. Where the blood-soaked causeways had run, broad avenues were laid out. Timber was stripped from the mountain sides to make roof beams for the Spanish houses, and lava rock was dug from the slopes of the volcanoes to make building blocks. Drainage ditches were dug and the broad lake that had surrounded and protected Tenochtitlán became a shallow pond, dry and dusty in the winter months.

Cortés the soldier became Cortés the ruler. The Spanish court, after much confusion, finally ig-

nored the protests of the Cuban governor, Diego Velásquez, and recognized Cortés as the supreme authority in the land that he had conquered. He sent expeditions in all directions to find the limits of the new land, hoping always to find a navigable channel to the Pacific and the Far East.

Cortés gave allotments of land and Indian slaves to his followers and built great estates for himself. Rude soldiers became men of wealth, owning vast plantations and ranches. Marina, the Indian girl without whose help the Spaniards never could have conquered, married one of Cortés' followers and became a lady of property and wealth.

Cuauhtemoc, the last brave defender of Tenochtitlán, remained a prisoner of the Spaniards. He was treated as a prince, but was not trusted. The Spaniards were always fearful of an Indian uprising, and the Aztecs who had survived the great siege still regarded Cuauhtemoc as their leader. Eventually the Aztec prince was executed for alleged treasonous activity while accompanying Cortés on an expedition into Central America.

Cortés was followed by other Spanish rulers and Mexico remained a Spanish colony for almost three centuries. New crops were introduced, horses and cattle were imported and great haciendas established. Mines for gold and silver were opened. The country was rich and the conquered Indians provided a vast supply of labor.

Finally, in 1810, Mexico rebelled against Spanish rule. The war that was to bring independence to Mexico eventually embroiled the entire nation.

But it started with the revolt of a humble parish priest named Father Hidalgo who had long grieved over the injustice with which the Spanish rulers had treated the Indians. Disobeying Spanish law, he had taught his Indian parishioners the cultivation of new crops and new ways of making leather and pottery.

With his friends Father Hidalgo had talked of rebellion against the governors sent out from Spain to rule them. When word came that the plotters were to be arrested, Father Hidalgo rang the bell of his church in the little town of Dolores, summoning his Indian parishioners. The time had come, he told them, to overthrow the Spanish governors.

Starting with his own followers, Father Hidalgo marched across the country toward Mexico City. Everywhere his revolutionary band was joined by more Indians, field and ranch hands, laborers from the gold and silver mines, mule drivers, woodsmen. They were armed only with knives, axes, slings and stones, little more than the weapons the Aztecs had used against Cortés and his men. And like the Aztecs before them, they were fierce, relentless and completely fearless. Some tried to stop the Spanish artillery fire by dashing forward and holding their straw sombreros over the mouth of the cannon. They fell by the hundreds, but for a time the weight of their numbers made them victorious.

This first flare-up of rebellion was, in time, quelled. Spanish soldiers executed Father Hidalgo and stuck his head on a wooden pike, to be exhibited as a warning to others who might rebel.

But the fire of rebellion did not die. In time

the descendants of Montezuma and Cuauhtemoc joined forces with the descendants of the Spanish conquerors who had followed Cortés, and together they threw off the rule of Spain and worked together to make Mexico a modern, independent nation.

About the author of this book:

WILLIAM JOHNSON first thought of writing a book about Cortés in 1931. As a student he traveled throughout Mexico and later, when he was a foreign correspondent there, he visited many of the famous places touched on by the Cortés expedition, such as Yucatán and Vera Cruz. Thus he approached his subject with a great and long-felt interest. Mr. Johnson writes: "Although I have worked as a war correspondent and foreign correspondent in many parts of the world, no other country holds as much fascination for me."

William Johnson is the author of another Landmark entitled, *Sam Houston, The Tallest Texan.* He was born and educated in Illinois and at the present time lives in California.

About the illustrator of this book:

JOSE CISNEROS was born in Mexico, but he has been a naturalized American citizen since 1948, living in Texas since 1934. From his childhood, history has always fascinated Mr. Cisneros — particularly in relation to costume — hence his interest in the graphic portrayal of it.

Although a self-taught artist, Jose Cisneros has developed his style by reading and by constantly observing the work of America's great illustrators, past and present. He is the illustrator of many books.

INDEX

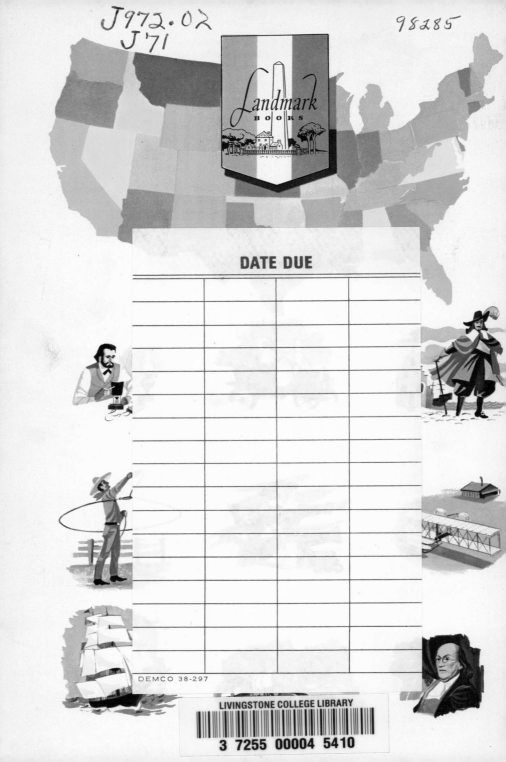